Walking
the Brecon Beacons and
the Black Mountains

David Hunter

D1419954

Published by Sigma Leisure – an imprint of

Sigma Press, 1 South Oak Lane, Wilmslow, Cheshire SK9 6AR, England.

British Library Cataloguing in Publication Data

A CIP record for this book is available from the British Library.

ISBN: 1-85058-474-5

Typesetting and Design by: Sigma Press, Wilmslow, Cheshire.

Cover photograph: the author on the summit of Fan y Big, in the Brecon Beacons

Photography: David & Vera Hunter

Maps: Vera Hunter

Printed by: MFP Design and Print

Contents

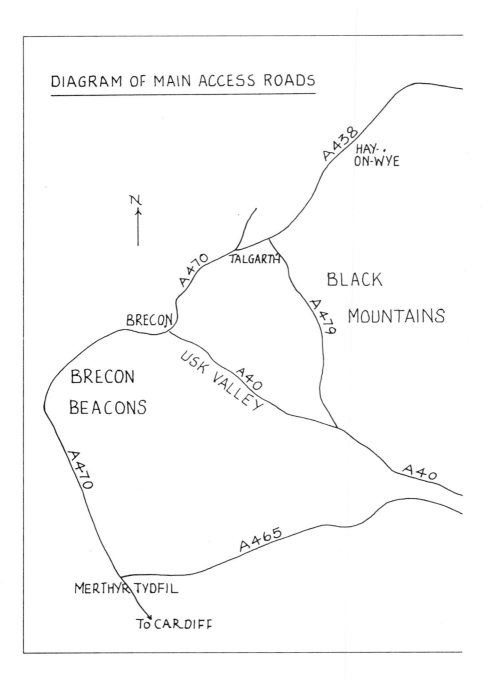

DIAGRAM OF MAIN ACCESS ROADS

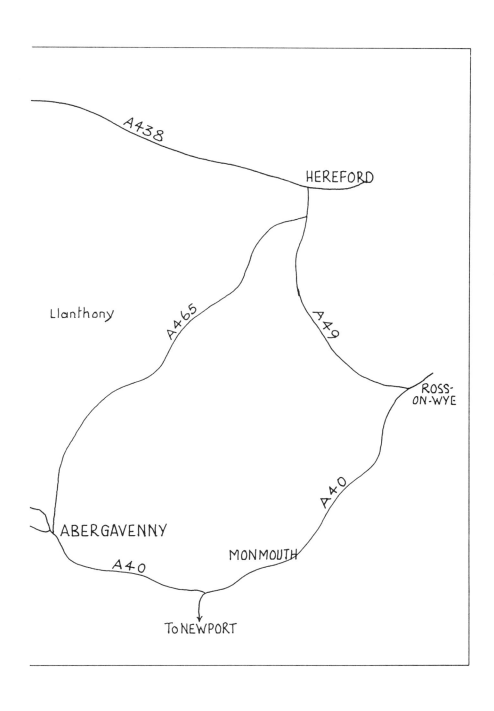

A Cautionary Note!

Readers are advised that many of the walks within this book are in high and sometimes remote country with some rough terrain. Weather conditions may change rapidly, accidents do occur from time to time and it is not impossible to get lost. The usual precautions of upland walking should be observed, including: the carrying of a map, compass, adequate food and drink, extra clothing, first-aid kit and survival bag.

While care has been taken in the preparation of this book, neither the author nor the publisher will accept any responsibility for errors or omissions, nor for any loss, accident or injury howsoever caused.

Maps

The Ordnance Survey has carried out a major re-mapping program in recent years. The Brecon Beacons are now accommodated on two sheets rather than three and have been extended: Outdoor Leisure 12 for the west and central areas and Outdoor Leisure 13 for the eastern area. This edition reflects these changes.

David Hunter

Introduction

The Welsh border country through the Black Mountains, the Vale of Usk and onward to the Brecon Beacons provides magnificent walking with routes which can be tailored to suit all abilities. It is this flexibility that has been a consideration in assembling the walks featured in these pages. The selection of circuits of between three and thirteen miles still leaves opportunities for those of an independent turn of mind to devise their own routes as they become acquainted with the hills. The area to be explored has been divided into four sections with a short introduction to each.

A view of the Brecon Beacons from the A40, near Brecon

1. The central area of the Brecon Beacons

This is contained within a roughly heart-shaped box bounded in the north by the A40 between Talybont-on-Usk and Brecon; the eastern boundary follows the narrow and highly scenic road running south-west from Talybont-on-Usk via a series of reservoirs to Pontsticill. The third enclosing road is the A470 running south from Brecon.

The highest peaks are in this area, with Pen y Fan (2907 ft) and its companions accessible from the car park within a couple of hours of steady walking by good paths. The west to east passage along the north-facing scarp of the Beacons linking Corn Du, Pen y Fan, Cribyn and Fan y Big is a rewarding switchback providing magnificent views. The direct ascent from the large car parks on the A470 ensures that these paths are well populated at least as far as Cribyn.

Less busy, but no less exciting approaches are made by narrow paths following craggy edges from the south and ridges that rise from the tangle of lanes on the north. While from the east a long trek over moorland via Twyn Du, Carn Pica and Waun Rydd provides a walk of different character. Beyond these self-imposed limits, excursions westwards are included to explore the waterfalls in the Ystradfellte area and the Craig Cerrig-gleisiad Nature Reserve just within the boundary of Fforest Fawr.

2. The tow-paths of the Monmouthshire and Brecon Canal

Moving eastwards, these lie in the Usk Valley and provide level sections for walks between Talybont and the architecturally interesting village of Crickhowell.

3. The Abergavenny area

The busy market town of Abergavenny looks over the Usk with the castle ramparts affording an excellent view to the surrounding hills. In this area the Sugar Loaf, Ysgyryd Fawr and the Blorenge all provide memorable walks.

4. The Black Mountains

These are not to be confused with the Black Mountain at the western extreme of the National Park. A series of walks takes full advantage of the long, striding moorland ridges and views that extend over a wide area of both England and Wales. Walks in this area include the twin peaks of Hay Bluff and Twmpa, Llanthony Priory and sections of the Offa's Dyke Path. Other excursions take paths climbing out of the Mynydd Du Forest, the iron age fort of Castell Dinas and to Waun Fach – at 2660 ft, the highest point of the Black Mountains.

* * *

Throughout, we are in a landscape that owes its appearance to both man and nature. Nature has provided the drama with the sculptured mountains, the deeply incised and beautifully wooded river gorges of the limestone country. She has dressed her creation in grass, heather, bracken and bilberry; a green landscape in the high days of summer turning to a blaze of rich colour with the arrival of autumn and lingering to brighten winter days.

Most of the area being explored is within Wales and the Brecon Beacons National Park, but a remote and delightful corner of Herefordshire is included with an outstanding ridge walk over Black Hill.

Man has left his signature in many ways: castles, hill top camps, and the regular patterning of the field enclosures seen to advantage from the hills. River valleys have been dammed to ensure the continuity of a good supply of water for industrial and domestic use, during which the engineers have created a mini Lake District. The demand for timber has seen the addition of large areas of coniferous forest, which climb the slopes in orderly fashion but happily do not completely overwhelm the landscape. Many forest roads are open to walkers as are some dismantled railway lines, old tramways and canal tow-paths.

The Terrain and Preparations for Walking

Most of the routes explore high mountain and moorland country where the usual common sense requirements of upland walking should be observed, for the mountains have many moods. One day they are kind and welcoming hosts inviting all to share in the glory of its blue skies and gentle breezes. On another, when the mist closes in trailing long white wraithes to clothe the hills in an insubstantial but impenetrable cloak of mystery, it forbids an invasion of its privacy, making it a secret place. An alien land where paths may be all too easily lost. The kindly breezes that cooled the heat of a summer day may give way to a fierce wind, with much energy expended in

Youth group from Outdoor Adventure Centre on the Brecon Beacons

battling against its icy blast.

All this is the stuff of high drama – a shade over the top you may think; but it serves to underline the oft-repeated advice to intending hill walkers to be properly equipped and to walk within their capabilities. In this context being properly equipped includes boots with good ankle support and grip, wet weather gear, spare warm clothing, not forgetting gloves, woolly bobble hat (or sun hat) survival bag, first aid kit, map and compass, whistle and torch. Take change, food for the day, with the addition of emergency rations and adequate liquid refreshment – heavy as it is to carry, it is important not to skimp on this in hot weather. In the shorter days of autumn and winter ample time should be allowed to complete the walk in daylight.

There is no close season for walking, but the latest weather forecast must be taken into account before embarking on any excursion into the hills, whatever the time of year.

Wayfinding, Maps and Compass Work

It is strongly recommended that the walk description should be read from start to finish before setting out. While brief summaries are given in the headings, no times are shown; this should be estimated from your own experience and preferred pace. Allowance being made for activities along the way, photography, bird watching, refreshment breaks and so on which can add considerable time to a rule of thumb calculation, of say, two miles an hour. In this connection there is an oft quoted measure of two and half miles an hour plus one hour for every fifteen hundred feet of height climbed. Only you can judge how well this works in practice.

The sketch maps that accompany each walk are for guidance only and are no substitute for the Ordnance Survey map, which should always be carried. While care has been taken to provide an accurate as possible a description, it should be used with the OS map.

Reference to north, generally westwards, east of south etc., are intended to be used only as indicators. Walkers should hold themselves responsible for taking their own accurate compass bearings from the map as required, not forgetting to allow for the appropriate magnetic variation. Practice in clear weather is never a wasted exercise and should help resolve any doubts that may arise in the interpretation of the text. Many of the approaches to the hills are waymarked out of the valleys but should not be followed slavishly since some may indicate circular routes established by the park authority. Cairns on the summit ridges are useful indicators of sometimes indistinct junctions of paths but in the absence of signposts, (the rule rather than the exception) the precise interpretation lies with the walker.

If you are walking in a group, large or small, make sure that a competent person has assumed responsibility for navigating. Many of the paths are obvious, and easy to follow over firm ground with no problems of wayfinding in clear weather. Others are less distinct with soggy patches to be dodged round from time to time but with no real terrors. Heavy rain and low cloud can snatch away reliable landmarks and give rise to uncertainty. Keep check of your position throughout the walk and be ready to make use of the compass **before** you are overtaken by bad weather. However fit and well-equipped you may be, accidents can happen in good weather as well as bad. It is a wise precaution, especially for those travelling alone, to leave a note of their intended route and expected time of return with some responsible person.

Each route is referenced with the appropriate maps. The preferred scale for walking is 1:25,000, i.e. 2½ inches to the mile. All the walks will be found on Outdoor Leisure Maps 12 and 13, Brecon Beacons National Park. Rights of way are shown in green on these sheets with some permissive paths picked out in brown. Many other paths are dotted in, but not all. In the upland areas there are many well-used paths which are not strictly speaking rights of way, some of these do not appear on the 1:25,000 sheets at the time of writing. The 1:50,000 Landranger Sheets 160 and 161, although smaller in scale and lacking some of the detail which it is possible to include on the 1:25,000, do include some tracks that may be absent from the larger sheets. Maps are continuously updated and I have noted the inclusion of additional information on new editions that have appeared since this book was first started.

The National Trust and the Brecon Beacons National Park own large tracts of hill country; Welsh Water and the Forestry Commission are equally welcoming to walkers, as are some landowners. The vast majority of paths over the hills can therefore be enjoyed whether they are a legal right of way or not. If this relaxed state of affairs is to continue, walkers and others engaged in outdoor leisure activities should keep in mind their own responsibilities in the countryside: Keep dogs under control, close gates, leave no litter, avoid disturbance to livestock or crops and generally behave in a considerate manner. To reasonable people it seems ridiculous to have to say all this, but unfortunately the unthinking or selfish conduct of a few makes it necessary.

Footpaths, public, permissive or otherwise may be closed or diverted to protect the countryside or livestock at sensitive times of the year – the lambing season, logging operations or periods of high fire risk. Clearly it is not practical for maps or books to take such changes into account so that walkers should be prepared to make suitable amendments to routes as the need arises.

Family Walking

The adventure of a day in the hills can be enjoyed to the full by quite young children. Don't spoil the day for you and them by selecting a route which may be beyond their capacity. Interest them in the things seen along the way, when the time is right teach them the basic use of map and compass. If infants are to be carried papoose fashion it is important to ensure that they are properly protected from the sun. Likewise their inactivity may, in windy conditions, cause the onset of hypothermia even in summer. Regular checks on their well-being, particularly when changes in weather conditions, angle of sun, etc., are noted should be a part of your outdoor routine.

If you are a newcomer to hill walking, do not be put off by the points that have been aired in the last few pages. They soon become second nature and can only serve to enhance your enjoyment of the hills in safety.

The Brecon Beacons

The Beacons lie a few miles south of the former county town of Brecon, offering an airy landscape that can be enjoyed by walkers of all abilities and ages. These grassy hills are sculptured with steep scalloped faces to the north, giving fine views to Brecon and the Black Mountains. To the south, the prospect extends for thirty miles to the Bristol Channel and beyond to the heights of Exmoor.

Access is easy with ample car parking, toilets and refreshments at Pont ar Daf on the A470 south-west of Brecon with further parking available at Storey Arms. There are car parks near the reservoirs and forest areas and are noted on the Ordnance Survey's Outdoor Leisure Map number 12 which covers the west and central areas of the Brecon Beacons National Park. Car parking space is rather less generous on the northern approaches and consequently attracts fewer casual walkers, but the routes are no less attractive and may well be preferred.

Though this is mountain country with the highest point in the range, Pen y Fan at 2907 ft, walking is relatively easy. A steady climb from the road with a final steep pitch or the mildest of scrambles is all that is needed to reach the tops. A succession of peaks run switchback fashion roughly from west to east with clear paths following the scarp edge over Corn Du, 2864 ft, Pen y Fan, Cribyn 2607 ft and Fan y Big, 2358 ft; these and others provide many options for exploring the hills.

On a fine summer day it seems that the world and his wife are here. Young men from the Junior Leaders Regiment making a fast and demanding traverse of the Fans, ramblers' groups with many members in their sixties but still young in heart, family parties ranging from five year-olds to grandfathers, well-equipped backpackers and picnickers with plastic bags. All may be found here and clearly enjoying every minute of their own particular adventure.

Inevitably, a penalty has been exacted from such popularity for

The Brecon Beacons through the doorway of Brecon Cathedral

boots are wearing out the mountains quicker than the mountains are wearing out boots. At least that is how it must seem to the National Trust team charged with the responsibility of putting right the severe erosion that has occurred in places. It is a long and painstaking task with materials being taken off the mountain to ensure a proper blending of the landscape. The damaged areas are being pitch paved, using techniques known to the Romans; water is culverted away and netting put on the surface to hold soil in place, allowing seeded grass to take hold. Once a firm path has been restored, the need for walkers to make an ever-widening and unsightly scar to avoid the worst of the erosion is removed and the mountain quickly recovers.

Brecon offers a good base from which to start an exploration of the Beacons and the gentler walking that is a feature of the Usk Valley. Like so many market towns it developed under the protection of a Norman castle, which has had a part to play not only in the history of the town but of the country at large. The town was laid out long before consideration for the needs of the motorist was required and presents a pleasant network of not over wide streets. You may expect it to be at its busiest on Market Days – Tuesday and Friday. An excellent town trail which picks out many architectural and historical points of interest is available from the Tourist Information Centre at the Cattle Market close to the main car park.

The castle was built in 1093 by Bernard of Newmarch to secure the area against the Welsh whose opposition to the Norman conquest was to extend into succeeding centuries.

It was this first Norman lord who was responsible for the foundation of the Priory church which, since 1923, has served as the cathedral for the diocese. It survived the dissolution of the monasteries by its continuance as the parish church of Brecon. The cathedral repays a visit with some features of interest briefly noted here. Among them is a large sixteenth-century carved cabinet of Flemish design. Nearby is the Cordwainers chapel with stained glass windows depicting three Lords of Brecknock: Humphrey de Bohan, Giles de Braos and Edward Stafford, Duke of Buckingham, the last Lord of Brecknock. The Harvard chapel is bedecked with the colours of one of the most famous regiments of the British army, the South Wales Borderers, together with the roll of honour of the 5777 officers and men who died during the 1914-18 war and those who, only twenty years later, were also called to war and destined not to return.

The forebears of these fighting men are recalled at the back of the cathedral by a stone once used for sharpening arrows; an explanatory note speculates on its use by the famed Welsh archers who did so much to carry the day at Agincourt. Nearby is another stone – the Cresset stone – with hollowed recesses to hold candles, an early chandelier and believed to be the largest in existence.

A wooden carving of a slender and elegant lady is all that remains of a memorial to the Games family, presumed to have been destroyed during the Cromwellian period. The archway of the south door provides a perfect framework for a view to the Brecon Beacons, a prospect which improves as you advance into the small garden which lies beyond.

The castle ruins are not available for inspection. One of its involuntary residents was John Morton, Bishop of Ely, who was held captive following his arrest by Richard III. The bishop was in the charge of the then Duke of Buckingham who seems to have been persuaded to his point of view leading to his involvement in an unsuccessful rebellion and inevitable execution. Morton, an astute man by all accounts, escaped to the continent, returning after Richard's death on Bosworth field, to serve as Archbishop and as Henry VII's Chancellor.

Brecon residents who have achieved fame include the actress Sarah Siddons, born at the Shoulder of Mutton Inn, now renamed in her honour. Another local worthy destined for wider fame was Sir David Gam who, with a small group of archers, fought with such distinction under Henry V at Agincourt. Gam was born David Llewellyn, a not uncommon name; he was distinguished from others carrying the same name by the reference to his squint – Gam – and the name stuck. Mortally wounded, he was knighted as he lay dying on the battlefield and there is a belief that Shakespeare used him as the model for Fluellen in Henry V.

Other places of interest include the Brecknock Museum, and the Museum of the South Wales Borderers.

The Brecon Beacons – Walk One:
Corn Du and Pen y Fan

Starting Point: Pont ar Daf car park off the A470, 7 miles south-west of Brecon. Toilets and picnic site.

Distance: 5 miles.

Detail: Steady climb on clear paths with fine views from summits of Corn Du and Pen y Fan.

Map: 1:25,000 Ordnance Survey Outdoor Leisure Map No. 12.

The direct route to Corn Du and Pen y Fan starts from the car park – a busy path on a fine Sunday so that the quieter route from Storey Arms is preferred for the outward leg of the circuit with the Pont ar Daf path used for the return.

The Walk

From the car park, head northwards along the A470 for half a mile to the Storey Arms – now an Outdoor Education Centre. Just beyond the centre there is a telephone box opposite a layby.

It should be noted that there are two possible routes to Corn Du from here. The first more clearly shown on the map with the familiar green dashes heads east of north to pass over the summit of Y Gyrn (2030 ft), swings to the east then south- east to reach the scarp above Llyn Cwm Llwch and thence to Corn Du. (Please see notes at the end of this chapter for further detail). Our route takes a more direct line reaching the scarp edge at a higher level and a little further to the south-east. While the map shows this as the faintest of dotted lines which seemingly comes to a halt when it reaches the Blaen Taf Fawr stream, there is a good clear path throughout. Subsequent revisions of the map will no doubt show the continuance of this well used way beyond the stream.

Take the track beyond the five barred gate, immediately passing the National Trust sign with a plantation and the Education Centre to your right. As the plantation falls back, your direction is generally north-easterly on an easy path, with the hillside covered in tufted grass. As you reach the top of the first rise, the flat topped summit of Corn Du is seen forward, half right.

Corn Du (left) and Pen y Fan from Cribyn

Continue climbing with the cleft through which the Blaen Taf Fawr tumbles to your right. The path falls to a fence — an old broken stone wall with toothy gaps reinforced by a wire fence. Once over the stile continue your descent, ignore the north/south crossing path and go on to cross the stream. The path now rises steadily to reach the scarp edge of Craig Cwm Llwch in a little under three-quarters of a mile.

Sheep graze the hillsides and you may see a shepherd rounding up his flock on horseback. It is a rewarding experience watching man and dog work together – strange calls and sharp whistles carried on the wind to the walker. A language that dog and man un-

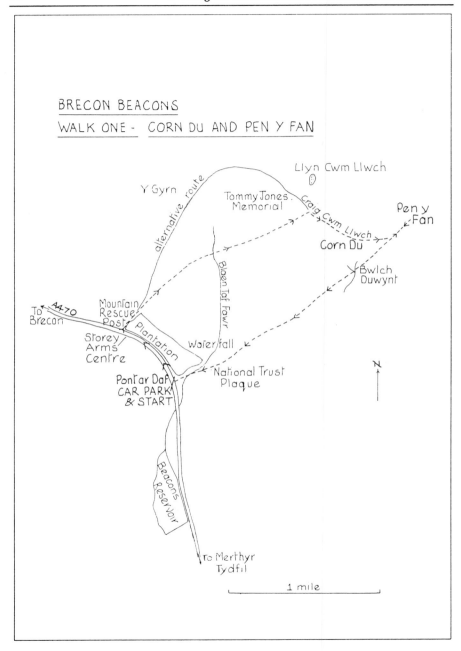

derstand to perfection. The reaction is swift, so much so that you are left wondering if it is thought transference rather than audible signals, so quickly does the dog obey the shepherd's bidding.

Not only sheep but hardy Welsh ponies graze the slopes under Corn Du. They make a marvellous subject for the camera with long tails, flowing manes and a wide range of colouring – brown, white, cream, grey and dappled – with the foals prancing and bucking for the sheer joy of living. But they are timid creatures – too close an approach will have them moving off and your picture may be lost.

The scarp edge gives a fine view down to the little grey eye of the hills – Llyn Cwm Llwch – around which an attractive path climbs to join the way to Corn Du. It passes close to the obelisk which recalls a tragedy at the beginning of the century when a five-year-old boy, Tommy Jones, was lost on the mountains and despite an extensive search his body was not found for several weeks.

The heavy traffic of boots along the edge, as elsewhere has done considerable damage to the pathway, but repair work by the National Trust has greatly improved the situation.

Turn right to follow the scarp edge with the full splendour of the sharp-edged, table-topped Corn Du seen to perfection with the near sheer fall to the north. Ignore the paths that swing away from Corn Du and continue taking the rocky steps on the left which bring you onto the summit cairn – 2864 ft – and the invigorating panorama of the hills. At the edge of Corn Du there is a fine flat rock from which photographers can compose their pictures of Pen y Fan. Viewing done and picture taking over, drop down the steep slope to follow the well-worn track to the twin peak of Pen y Fan, the highest point in the Beacons, 2907 ft.

Viewed from the north the saddle between the two is supposed to represent a giant arm chair and although not so marked on the map has long been known as Arthur's Chair. As far back as 1189, Gerald of Wales, refers to it as such and to a local tradition that the hills were owned by the legendary king.

On a clear day the views are wide ranging. Near at hand, to the east is the next inviting peak, Cribyn, beyond which can be seen the distant but shapely Sugar Loaf near Abergavenny. To the south, the glint of sun on the reservoir and, far away, another silvered thread of water – the Bristol Channel and beyond, the hills of Somerset.

Jet black ravens glide effortlessly under the northern slopes of the Beacons riding the thermals with consummate ease. A skill that man has long envied and now emulates in gliders that swish along the Beacon tops. The sheep that roam these hills are far less timid than the ponies.Some are positively aggressive once a party of walkers sits down and the rustle of sandwich bags is heard.

To continue the walk, retrace your steps over the summit of Pen y Fan and head back towards Corn Du. When the track divides, take the left fork that leads under its slopes to the poetically named Bwlch Duwynt, Pass of the Black Wind – half a mile south-west of Pen y Fan, where a path comes in from the ridge of Craig Gwaun Taf.

From Bwlch Duwynt, a wide clear track descends to reach the car park at Pont ar Daf in a mile and a quarter with very little need for any further route description.

This is another path which had suffered severely from erosion and at its lower levels the restoration work has virtually produced a paved path, intersected by open culverts. As you draw level with the edge of a conifer plantation seen away to your right a streamlet is crossed. Just beyond is a small pillar with an inscription that records "The Brecon Beacons were given to the National Trust by the Eagle Star Insurance Company in 1965."

On the right is the cleft through which the Blaen Taf Fawr runs, now a little wider having collected contributions from several of its fellows on its way down the hillside. (It goes on to flow through the Beacons, Cantref and Llwyn-on reservoirs from which it emerges as the Afon Taf Fawr).

The path runs down to a ford and stepping stones, then to a five-barred gate and a path leads through trees to the car park.

The virtues of the alternative route taking in Y Gyrn include an excellent view to the Beacons, an inspection of the Tommy Jones memorial obelisk and a bird's eye prospect of Llyn Cwm Llwch.

The Brecon Beacons – Walk Two: Pen y Fan via Cribyn

Starting Point: Cwmcynwyn – 3½ miles from Brecon and approached by the Bailihelig Road. No facilities and space for only a few cars at the end of the lane – careful parking essential.

Distance: 7½ miles (for a shorter alternative, see Walk Three).

Detail: A steady climb on an easy path to the top of the pass which provides excellent views of the steep northern faces of the Beacons, thence a switch-back over Cribyn along the scarp edge to Pen y Fan with a long and enjoyable descent.

Map: 1:25,000 Ordnance Survey Outdoor Leisure Map No 12.

Some of the paths over the Beacons are not old routes trodden by travellers over the centuries but more recent, made by walkers during the last fifty years as taking to the hills has become an increasingly popular recreation. Not so the outward route of this circuit which is a very old road indeed, the gradients kind to both walkers and packhorses and nowadays finding favour with mountain bikers. Nobody seems to know quite how old it is but it is sometimes referred to as the Roman Road.

The Walk

The narrow metalled lane from Brecon comes to an abrupt end by the private road to Cwmcynwyn and cars can go no further. Ahead lies an uncomfortably rocky road which is followed for 200 yards between hedges to emerge onto the open hillside.

Ignore the obvious route up the ridge of Bryn Teg and go forward following the line of the stone wall on your left. At the end of the wall ignore the path that continues diagonally left along the fence line and continue uphill on your broad track. Ahead will be seen the nick in the hills marked on the

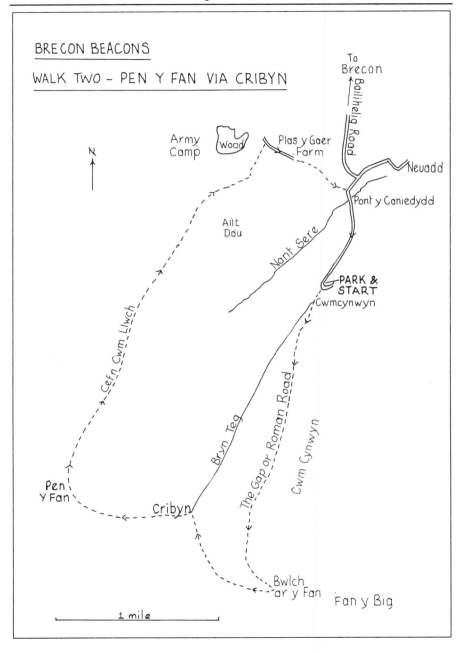

BRECON BEACONS

WALK TWO – PEN Y FAN VIA CRIBYN

To Brecon

Bailihelig Road

N

Army Camp

Wood

Plas y Gaer Farm

Neuadd

Pont y Caniedydd

Ailt Ddu

Nant Sere

PARK & START
Cwmcynwyn

Cefn Cwm Llwch

Bryn Teg

The Gap or Roman Road

Cwm Cynwyn

Pen Y Fan

Cribyn

Bwlch ar y Fan

Fan y Big

1 mile

on your broad track. Ahead will be seen the nick in the hills marked on the map as Bwlch ar y Fan – pass (or gap) on the peak. It is more conveniently called The Gap, from which our way derives its other name, The Gap Road.

The road follows as clear a way as you are likely to find, rising steadily and a little west of south for two miles to The Gap, the dip between Fan y Big, 2359 ft, on the east and the scarp of Craig Cwm which rises to Cribyn to the west.

As you make your way along the track the long ridge of Bryn Teg is to your right. On the left the ground falls away to the, at first, wooded Cwm Cynwyn with its attendant stream. Beyond, the slopes rise steeply to the long ridge of Cefn Cyff leading to the summit of Fan y Big. From one angle Fan y Big presents a partial sphinx-like image. The upper section of the Gap Road can be wet underfoot as several springs rise on the sides of Bryn Teg and spill across the path to join the Nant Cynwyn 400 ft below. The underlying rocks are tinged with green and diminutive walkers on the Bryn Teg route can be seen making the last steep ascent that carries them to the summit of Cribyn.

The road tops at 1965 ft, a good spot to pause and take a last look back down the track. You can also trace the long twisting passage of the Nant Cynwyn from under Fan y Big until it disappears into the oak trees of the lower valley. Soon after leaving the trees it merges with the Nant Sere to continue as the Afon Cynrig, it too, soon loses its identity as it merges with the waters of the Usk near Brecon.

The Gap Road continues its way southwards towards the Taf Fechan Forest and the Neuadd Reservoir is seen shimmering below. But our way swings sharply right at the top of the pass to climb steeply along the edge of Craig Cwm Cynwyn, gaining a further 653 feet of height in the three-quarters of a mile it takes to reach the summit of Cribyn.

The view does not disappoint. East and west, the sharp table-topped summits of the Beacons; to the north, Brecon sits in its farming landscape; to the south, the far views which are to be enjoyed again from Pen y Fan, with the dark green of the forest pines running down to the blue waters of the reservoirs. Pen y Fan can look its best from Cribyn, balanced by the more distant Corn Du. Where it drops away to the north, it resembles a giant layer cake that has been recklessly sliced through, rocky crumbs tumbling down the bands of red where the sandstone shows through the thin grass.

Onward from Cribyn along the edge of the scarp; 425 feet of height are quickly lost then 725 feet added as Craig Cwm Sere is traversed with one last steep scramble to Pen y Fan.

Again the views are high, wide and handsome extending southwards to the Bristol Channel, eastwards to the Sugar Loaf and – on a good day – to the nine-mile ridge of Elgar's beloved Malvern Hills. To the west the groups of walkers on Corn Du recall the familiar film shots of Red Indians gathering on the rocks of Monument Valley. On the ridge of Craig Gwaun Taf, slow-moving silhouettes offer an unspoken invitation to further days on the hills. From Cribyn we admired the proud face of Pen y Fan, now the compliment can be returned from the flat rock step at the eastern end of Pen y Fan.

The return journey starts from the summit. Take the path immediately to the north of the triangulation point to make a steep scrambling drop on a rocky eroded path for a hundred feet or so before easing out to a more comfortable descent. To the right Cribyn assumes almost pyramid proportions, the once green Pen y Fan may now assume a dark and brooding aspect. In the far distance, half right, the waters of Llangorse lake catch the sun.

A long level passage is made along Cefn Cwm Llwch in the general direction of Brecon with the companion ridge of Bryn Teg across the valley to the right. The path descends again and a little below the ridge a secondary path on the right provides shelter from the wind when required.

A mile and a quarter from Pen y Fan, the paths divide. Take care not to take the path which runs on to the disused quarries and Allt Ddu but follow the clearer bridle way that continues with the descent along its western flanks.

The Nissen huts of the army camp at Cwm Gwdi will be seen forward left. As you round the hill, marker posts head left but continue until the path leads naturally to the point of exit under the northern edge of Allt Ddu. The spot can be identified from the path; it is 200 yards to the east of the

Cribyn from Pen y Fan

woods which lie beyond the army camp, leaving the National Trust boundary by a five-barred gate.

The gate leads on to a hollow way, occupied to varying extents by a stream. Follow this east of north for 200 yards to a rough metalled lane. Turn right and you reach Plas y Gaer farm in 300 yards.

The path exits by the eastern gateway of the farm, then on to the metal gateway at the diagonal right corner of the field. Continue with the boundary on your right to a further gateway. Beyond this, follow the edge of the field with the boundary to your left, making for the metal gateway opposite. Once through the gate head down towards the farm buildings at Pant, pass through gateway and turn left along a stony track for 200 yards. On reaching a lane turn right and proceed for just over half a mile to return to your starting point.

The Brecon Beacons – Walk Three: Cribyn by The Gap

Starting Point: Cwmcynwyn – 3½ miles from Brecon and approached by the Bailihelig Road. No facilities and space for only a few cars at the end of the lane – careful parking essential.

Distance: 4¼ miles (for a longer alternative, see Walk Two).

Detail: A steady climb on an easy path to the top of the pass which provides an excellent view of the steep northern faces of the Beacons, thence a climb along the scarp edge to Cribyn with a descent by the Bryn Teg ridge.

Maps: 1:25,000 Ordnance Survey Outdoor Leisure Map No. 12.

This walk is a shortened version of the one described in Walk Two, so the scenic description has been largely omitted but the relevant walking directions are included for ease of reference.

The Walk

From the end of the lane take the rocky road southwards which in 200 yards emerges into the open landscape of the National Trust's Brecon Beacons estate.

Go forward with the stone wall to your left and, when this falls back, continue with The Gap Road to reach the top of the pass at Bwlch ar y Fan (1965 ft) with Fan y Big on your left.

Turn right to follow the rising scarp edge to reach the summit of Cribyn (2608 ft) with its all round prospect of the Beacons and the wide world beyond.

The return is now made by way of the Bryn Teg ridge, the path being found immediately north of the summit of Cribyn. A steep descent soon eases to provide a fine return to your starting point with good views.

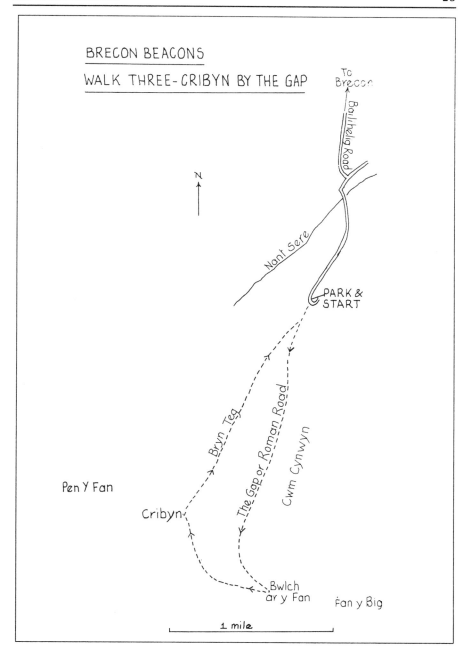

BRECON BEACONS

WALK THREE- CRIBYN BY THE GAP

To Brecon

Bailihelig Road

N

Nant Sere

PARK & START

Bryn Teg

The Gap or Roman Road

Cwm Cynwyn

Pen Y Fan

Cribyn

Bwlch ar y Fan

Fan y Big

1 mile

The Brecon Beacons – Walk Four: A Circuit of the Fans from the South

Starting Point: The Gap Road – half a mile south of the lower Neuadd Reservoir. Access from the A40 – leave at the turn for Talybont-on-Usk to Aber and follow the western side of the Talybont Reservoir until Neuadd is signposted on the right above Pentwyn Reservoir. Approach from A470 – take the road to Pontsticill then northwards along the western side of Pontsticill Reservoir to join Neuadd Road north of Pentwyn Reservoir.

Distance: 9 miles over the peaks or 8 miles if option taking the path under the summits.

Detail: An exposed but exhilarating circuit. A steep climb to follow the long ridge to Bwlch Duwynt, thence a switch-back route over three of the highest Beacons with a steady descent by The Gap Road.

Map: 1:25,000 Ordnance Survey Outdoor Leisure Map No 12.

Toilets: Nearest at Talybont-on-Usk.

This is an immensely enjoyable circuit but exposed to all the winds that blow and a clear day is essential for its maximum enjoyment. There is a car park in the Taf Fechan Forest at Pont Cwmyfedwen three-quarters of a mile south of the start point. Here after rain, the stream tumbles over its rocky bed in a satisfying commotion of white water. There is room to park a few cars off the road with discretion close to the starting point of the walk but at weekends and busy times the official car park should be used.

An alternative start can be made from the path on the left-hand side of the Neuadd Road (signed Lower Neuadd Reservoir) found about 300 yards south of the car park at Pont Cwmyfedwen. This would add about 1½ miles to the entire round but may be necessary if possible alteration work to the dam wall is put into effect.

A slightly indirect beginning to this walk is used to take advantage of the fine morning views to the Beacons before turning westwards to join the ridge that leads to the summits.

Walkers on Pen y Fan

The Walk

The Gap Road is joined half a mile south of the Lower Neuadd Reservoir on the right, signed `Unsuitable for Motor Vehicles' with a further plate, reminiscent of the London Underground, which reads `Mind the gap'. This wide and easy to follow track crosses the mountains north to south and is sometimes called The Roman Road.

Take the track with the forest to your right with magnificent views of the peaks unfolding as you advance. Left to right as the panorama is revealed: the table-topped Corn Du, a dip before the climb to Pen y Fan, a sweep down before rising again to the pointed summit of Cribyn, another sharp drop to the Gap Pass with Fan y Big being added to the east. In the foreground, the two Neuadd Reservoirs and, to the south of these, the Taf Fechan Forest climbs the valley slopes.

In just under half a mile a gate is met beyond which the track tumbles into the deep cleft cut by the Nant y Gloesydd. Once over the stream turn left to follow the path downhill towards the lower reservoir to meet and pass through a metal gate and over a track. Opposite is a narrow gap. Descend to a tarmac road, beware deep step, and turn left passing the old waterworks buildings. Shortly bear right descending on a curving path to cross the footbridge over the outlet and half left up the dam bank. Continue to leave by the gateway on the western side of the reservoir. The path through the forest mentioned as an alternative start joins the route at this point. Head up the hillside on a clear track which runs parallel with the outside edge of the forested area.

The views improve as height is gained. As the forest falls back, continue climbing. The upper approaches are steep and may be very wet under foot as water dribbles down the hillside; erosion has added to the need for care. The top of the slope is reached after 660 feet of ascent with the triangulation point seen about 200 yards to the south. Turn right, ie northwards, to follow the scarp edge for nearly two miles. At first the ground to your left is a rough grassy plateau but as progress is made it narrows to a distinct ridge. To your right the edge falls away with increasing sharpness until it becomes a sheer cliff.

The path, though narrow at times, is clearly defined and easy to follow, provided the not uncommon high winds allow you to stand upright. On such occasions, the wind hitting the stout walls of the mountain sounds like the sea breaking at the foot of rocky cliffs.

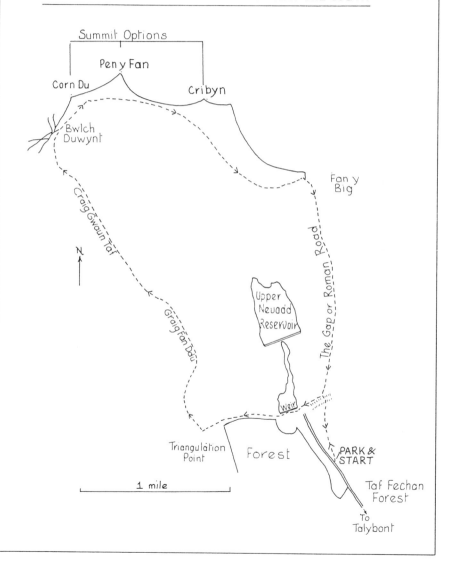

BRECON BEACONS

WALK FOUR– A CIRCUIT OF THE FANS FROM THE SOUTH

Summit Options

Pen y Fan

Corn Du

Cribyn

Bwlch Duwynt

Fan y Big

Craig Gwaun Taf

N

Craig Fan Ddu

Upper Neuadd Reservoir

The Gap or Roman Road

Weir

Triangulation Point

Forest

PARK & START

Taf Fechan Forest

1 mile

To Talybont

The passage is made along Graig Fan Ddu, and on to Rhiw yr Ysgyfarnog from which the deep scoop to your left is seen – Cwm Crew. You could well believe that a huge meteorite had struck here with devastating effect aeons ago. Peat is joined by outcropping rocks, ravens glide silently through the air in marked contrast to the military aircraft that may catch you off guard as they scream through the hills at terrifying speed. However, this can be a fine place to watch the shadows of the clouds chasing across the landscape, the dark green guardian pines fringing the blue waters of the reservoir and to look down upon the hardy hill ponies grazing far below.

Onward then, along Craig Gwaun Taf to reach the Bwlch Duwynt – the Pass of the Black Wind – named with considerable justification if you have battled against a howling gale for the last two miles.

Now is the time to consider the options for your further progress according to energy, inclination, weather conditions or simply the remaining hours of daylight that may be available. The choices are to take the not inconsiderable rise and fall over all three peaks, Corn Du, Pen y Fan and Cribyn, select one or two of them, or simply by-pass them all by taking the lower path that runs along their flanks to join the pass at Bwlch ar y Fan.

The Summits Option

From the end of the ridge swing to the right. Corn Du, looking very triangular, is seen ahead with an obvious path to the summit to set you on your way over the successive peaks.

If the Beacons look splendid from your southern approach then the prospect from the summits can only be described as dramatic with the sharply scalloped northern faces plunging hundreds of feet. The views are fine in all directions, Brecon almost lost in the landscape to the north, the Black Mountains in the eastern arc with the Sugar Loaf easily identified. To the south the gleaming waters of the Bristol Channel and beyond the black smudge that marks the high ground of Exmoor.

From the top of Corn Du (2864 ft) a well-worn track descends to the saddle and a climb is made to Pen y Fan, at 2907 ft the highest of the Beacons. From Pen y Fan a descent of 725 feet is made along the scarp edge of Craig Cwm Sere with 425 feet to be recovered to reach the summit of Cribyn. At 2608 ft, this is a lesser height but in no other way inferior. The last stage of the switchback is a three-quarters of a mile walk along the edge of Craig Cwm Cynwyn. There are superb views of the northern section of the Gap Road, as a descent is made to Bwlch ar y Fan — the Gap Pass — marking the return leg of this walk.

Further Options

If omitting the peaks, or saving your energies for Pen y Fan, bear right on the path under the southern flanks of Corn Du. This track heads north-easterly directly to Pen y Fan. As the track starts to rise towards the Fan, peak dodgers should watch for the narrower but clear path half right, which skirts under its southern heights. This connects with paths on the eastern slopes of Pen y Fan. As you approach the foot of Pen y Fan the paths clearly divide, one forking half left up to Cribyn, the other across the hillside. This lower path may provide an opportunity to see the hill ponies at closer quarters. Photographers hoping for good pictures should not approach too closely especially if there are foals in the group; patience and a zoom lens are likely to produce the best results.

Peak baggers will have descended from Cribyn by way of the sharp edge of Craig Cwm Cynwyn to the Gap Road under the great green pyramid of Fan y Big; the lower path also meets the road at this point. Swing right with the road making a clear and gentle descent of one and a half miles to the Taf Fechan Forest and the crossing of the Nant y Gloesydd. From here retrace the half mile of your outward journey to rejoin the tarmac road and your starting point.

The Brecon Beacons – Walk Five: Fan Y Big via Craig y Fan Ddu

Starting Point: The Forestry Commission car park on the forest edge at the western end of the Talybont Valley. Access from A40: via the minor road through Talybont-on-Usk, Aber, along the reservoir edge to the top of the valley where the car park is signposted on the right as the road emerges from the forest – an agreeable scenic route. Access from the A470: take the minor road to Pontsticill and northwards on the western side of Pontsticill and Pentwyn reservoirs following signs for Talybont. The car park is found on the left about half a mile after leaving the Taf Fechan Forest.

Distance: 8 miles.

Detail: An exposed and exciting circuit with an initial steep ascent but, after that, an easy to follow but less frequented way along miles of scarp edge. Clear weather is essential.

Map: 1:25,000 Ordnance Survey Outdoor Leisure Map No 12.

Toilets: Nearest – Aber camp site or Talybont-on-Usk.

This circuit is something of a connoisseur's walk to be enjoyed to the full when acquaintance has already been made with the main heights of the Brecon Beacons. They are viewed to advantage as the walk progresses. The route includes nearly five miles of continuous scarp edge walking with magnificent views, so pick the day for this expedition with care.

The car park, with one at a lower level to the east, gives access to a short waterfall walk provided by the Forestry Commission. This can be explored if time allows or remembered for another occasion.

The Walk

From the car park, return the short distance to the edge of the forest. After crossing a cattle grid and a stream (two mini-waterfalls) take the grassy

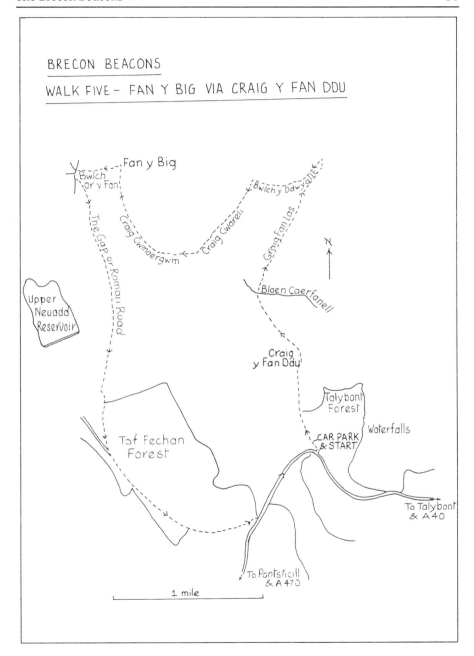

BRECON BEACONS

WALK FIVE - FAN Y BIG VIA CRAIG Y FAN DDU

crossing a cattle grid and a stream (two mini-waterfalls) take the grassy path on the right which climbs the hillside. In about 200 yards a path comes in from the left; turn right with this to cross the stream and then left to continue up the hillside with the forest fence to your right.

The stream lies deep in a cleft, tumbling over a series of minor waterfalls as it drains the peaty terrain, with modest clumps of primroses scattered here and there on its steep banks – in bloom as late as the first week in June. From the short cropped turf tiny yellow flowers stare back at the walker – tormentil – the herbalists made use of it in preparations to treat stomach disorders.

The views improve at every step, forward half right is the great scoop cut out of the eastern end of the Beacons range. The forest itself is set in a bowl of the hills, to the south its upper boundaries are seen gently curving like the shallow bays of a coastline. It can present the blackest of faces but sunlight reveals the full shade card of green. Beyond the first ridge are extensive quarry faces where limestone is cut out of the hill to make roadstone.

When the forest fence falls back continue climbing up the green hillside covered in rough grass and bilberry with your target the southern tip of Craig y Fan Ddu unmistakable. Forward and to the left the two highest of the Beacons appear – Corn Du and Pen y Fan. Leading up to them on the western horizon is the long scarp that broods over the Neuadd reservoirs which was explored in Walk Four.

As you approach the summit plateau the path divides, take the right fork which rounds the southern end and gives a brief glimpse of the Talybont Reservoir. From here, the walk follows the scarp edge on narrow but clear paths. Head north along the eastern edge of Craig y Fan Ddu with views of forest and mountain.

There is a sheer drop to your right as the plateau is abruptly cut off, with the weathered edges of stratified rocks protruding over the edge. Far below is a spider web of tiny streams as springs spill forth the precious gift of water stored within the mountain. A dozen more unnamed rivulets fall down the hillsides, their combined forces widening to become the Caerfanell. Soon its brief passage in the valley is halted as it helps swell the resources of the quarter of a mile wide, two-mile long Talybont reservoir. Released from its imprisonment, it flows on to lose its identity in the waters of the Usk.

A second track to your left and a few yards in from the very edge may provide some temporary relief from the blast of the east wind if the day proves less calm than expected.

At the end of Craig Fan y Ddu, the Beacons are again seen beyond an expanse of peaty moorland and, as a little more height is gained, the Taf Fechan Forest appears.

In nearly three-quarters of a mile after joining the scarp edge the path makes a small loop to round the deep cleft cut by the Blaen Caerfanell. Here there is a junction of paths with the stream conveniently crossed on slabs of flat rocks. Shortly after the stream, a spongy peat area has to be rounded, but the short loop soon returns to the scarp edge of Graig Fan Las with your direction now east of north. Now is the moment to look back to Craig y Fan Ddu, in late spring its eastern slopes falling to the valley as a huge green velvet curtain, rouched in theatrical style.

The scarp edge is followed for a further mile, Corn Du and Pen y Fan again peeping over the wide expanse of peat moorland, ragged, eroded — the land shedding an unwanted skin.

The grass-topped peat hillocks which remain rise eight feet above the general level with chunks several cubic feet in size being sloughed off. A strange, eerie landscape. Looking ahead to the north-east, the slopes of Waun Rydd exhibit a similar process of erosion. The ground is shaped to take on the outlines of a relief map – or maybe the lion's mane trimming of some fancy French poodle.

Nearing the end of Graig Fan Las, the path runs a little under the contour line with the view narrowing along the single file tread. Towards the end of the scarp a path is seen coming in over Waun Rydd and a narrow V gap ahead slowly opens up a view to the north. A crossroads of paths merges, a welcome meeting of ways familiar to hill walkers. From the north, the long route that has climbed from Pencelli over Rhiw Bwlch y Ddwyallt; from the east, the way that has trekked over Twyn Du, Carn Pica and Waun Rydd. Such meeting spots are where the maps come out and future walks are planned on promising-looking ridges.

Our way lies to the left gently curving westwards along the scarp edge of Bwlch y Ddwyallt.

To the left the weathered moorland of Gwaun Cerrig Llwydion, forsaken it seems by both man and nature, perhaps condemned to turn into an increasingly grassless upland desert. To the right the edge falls quickly away to be swallowed up in the depths of Cwm Cwareli. A minor unnamed ridge attempts to climb the scarp but fails to properly bridge the gap. Along the way we pass, imperceptibly, the highest point of the circuit, 2493 ft.

Half a mile from the meeting of the mountain ways a change of direction begins, a three-sided circumnavigation of the great crater that has been carved out of the mountain. Craig Cwareli is followed south-west for over half a mile, then the path heads west, looking over Cwm Oergwm and the long thin line of broad leaved woodland through which the Nant Menasgin falls. Closer by, looking back to Craig Cwareli, there are subtle colourings of shades of green, beige, with rocks of red, pink and grey.

For some time now the view to the north has been of shapely ridges and deep valleys leading down to a green chequer board of farmland which, in turn, rises steadily to fade away to a blue grey infinity of hills and sky. Westwards lies the drama, the sharp face of Cribyn with Pen y Fan rising beyond it, then the flat top of Corn Du, the heights telescoped together, with the lower ground out of sight for the moment. It is a view that those who only head for Pen y Fan by direct ways never see. But it is part of a great jigsaw, with many pieces to assemble in their exploration. A familiar peak seen from a new angle, a promising path discovered and noted for another day, a change in the season dressing the hills in different colours. The whole theatre of the landscape set to change the scene, brilliantly lit or with light and shade of the clouds playing hide and seek with the sun, the mountains now bright and open, now dark and mysterious.

The crater's edge changes direction again, north-west along Craig Cwmoergwm, then north. A final steady ascent over grassy slopes leads on to the 2358 ft Fan y Big, with its small summit cairn seen boldly ahead with the main peaks of the Fans now much closer.

Fan y Big is a fine pivotal point from which to enjoy the Beacons.

The view north includes Brecon almost lost in the surrounding farmland, with the Cefn Cyff ridge rising up to join us. The east is dominated by the deep cwms and the cliff edges we have travelled along and in the distance the Black Mountains. Somewhere between, a sudden jarring note in the symphony of colours – an unexpected splash of luminescent yellow – a faraway field of oil seed rape in full flower. To the west, a sheer drop followed by the steeply shelving slopes to Cwm Cynwyn, beyond which the Gap Road makes its way to the top of the pass. Above the Gap Road the Bryn Teg ridge with its final thrust to achieve the sharp nosed summit of Cribyn. Then Pen y Fan majestic as ever and behind Corn Du – a giant's table set out on the hills.

Having drunk your fill of the view, head back south along the edge and in a few yards take the path which makes a steep grassy 400 feet descent westwards to another meeting of ways at the top of the Gap Pass. (Shown on the map as Bwlch ar y Fan). Now turn left on the broad track, the Gap Road (or Roman Road), and follow this southwards for a mile and a half. The afternoon light frequently produces beautifully back-lit pictures of the blue waters of the Upper Neuadd Reservoir sparkling with its fringe of pines.

When the deep ravine cut by a stream is reached, pass through this to a gateway. Continue along the Gap Road with the forest to your left. On reaching the metalled lane, ignore it and take the broad fenced track immediately ahead which at first runs along the outside edge of the forest. Keep with the track passing through several gateways and in half a mile join a forest road.

Pursue the forest way for a further half mile and when sheep pens are met swing right to a minor road. Here turn left and in a little over half a mile turn left on a track to return to your starting point at the top end of the Talybont Forest.

The Brecon Beacons – Walk Six: Waterfalls Adventure

Starting Point: Forestry Commissions Porth yr Ogof car park about one mile south of Ystradfellte.

Access: leave the A470 about 1½ miles south of Storey Arms, taking the scenic A4059 at the southern end of the Beacons Reservoir. After 6 miles, turn right on a minor road; when this divides after 1 mile, take the left fork and, in just over half a mile, take the sharp left, easy to miss road, to reach a car park in little over half a mile.

Distance: 4¼ miles

Detail: A delightful and dramatic exploration of a series of waterfalls to the west of the Brecon Beacons over rough and steep terrain for which stout footwear and care are essential. Fatal accidents have occurred in the area. Having said this, with adult supervision of children, families can enjoy the advised route, the long stepped descent of the gorge and the excitement of walking behind a waterfall.

Map: Outdoor Leisure Map No. 12.

Toilets: At car park.

There are days when low clouds or the threat of persistent showers may keep walkers off the summits and less exposed territory must be found for a day's excursion. Just such a spot is the limestone country to the west of the Beacons where rivers flowing through deep, tree-clad gorges tumble down a series of delightful waterfalls. This walk is an ideal outing, a scenic route with some shelter afforded by the forest. It is right to repeat the warning already given above and which is emphasised by the succession of notices erected by the Forestry Commission, which could scarcely be more specific. "The gorges near the waterfalls are very dangerous and deaths have occurred, smooth soled shoes are very risky."

The route described includes a passage along the steep edge of the gorge on a narrow path, care is required. It should be noted that the Forestry Commission have provided a less hazardous way-marked path which leaves our route just beyond the footbridge.

The car park is sited at the point where the River Mellte disappears underground, swallowed up in the blackness of a great cavern, hence the name Porth yr Ogof which can be translated as The Door of the Cave. A suitably dramatic curtain raiser to this walk. An assembly of boiler-suited, hard-hatted pot-holers may be seen preparing to set off on their underground explorations – ours will be conducted strictly on the surface.

The Walk

From the car park go forward to cross the road and take the path directly ahead. Almost immediately, a hole in the rocks will be seen on your right, perhaps with a rope attached to some adjacent pipework – all that you may see of the pot-holers who have already disappeared into the bowels of the earth. A further pot-hole will be noted to the left. Continue to take the path beyond the triple stile – the only one I have seen and clear evidence of the popularity of this area.

The start is across an eroded pavement where the action of water and swirling pebbles have carved out a series of pudding-bowl like hollows which, when wet, make them even more slippery underfoot. The eastern bank of the Mellte is followed although, for the first quarter of a mile, it is out of sight until a rocky descent allows an inspection of the yawning black tunnel from which it now exits.

Beyond the first obstacle course lies the grassy Blue Pool picnic area. The river widens, with the path alongside, at first only a few feet above the water but later following a narrow edge with a substantial drop to the river.

A temporary respite provided by a smoother path gives an opportunity to enjoy the river and keep an eye open for dippers and wagtails. The rocks give way to stumbling tree roots as the path makes a way through broad leafed woodland, hazel, ash, sycamore and oak.

Beyond the wooded section a stile leads on to a marshy open area thick with rushes. Three-quarters of a mile from the start a footbridge is met. Our way remains on the eastern banks so its services are not required.

Sgwd Clun-gwyn waterfall, Afon Mellte

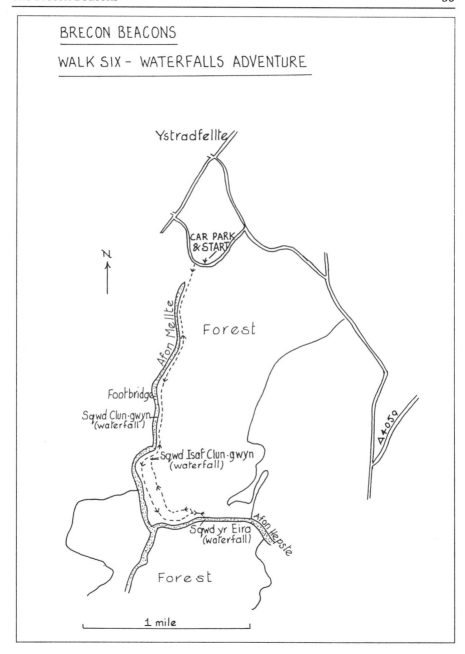

BRECON BEACONS

WALK SIX - WATERFALLS ADVENTURE

Ystradfellte

CAR PARK
& START

N

Afon Mellte

Forest

A4059

Footbridge

Sqwd Clun-gwyn
(waterfall)

Sqwd Isaf Clun-gwyn
(waterfall)

Afon Hepste

Sqwd yr Eira
(waterfall)

Forest

1 mile

Those taking the easier waymarked route may like to make a diversion over the bridge and continue downstream for 300 yards to get a view of the first waterfall which may otherwise be missed; but you will have to retrace your steps to rejoin the route.

Continuing on the eastern bank, a short scrambling ascent is made over rocks. The path now divides after only a short distance, keep to the riverside path for the moment – another warning notice appears.

When the rock table that precedes the waterfall of Sgwd Clun-gwyn is reached, take the stepped path, which is followed a few feet above the river. This is a narrow slippery way with, now and again, an interesting growth of fungus to be seen on the trees.

And so to the fall, where a rush of white water tumbles over twin ledges, to drop 35 feet after an initial stutter, with a crescendo of noise – the endless finale of a great symphony.

From the fall rejoin the path continuing downstream, immediately a trickle of water across the path puts on its own display as lemming like it drops over the cliff edge. The mix of woodland and water is superb as the river follows the ever deepening gorge.

Soon a waymark again directs walkers diagonally forward and left, away from the river with the legend "advised path to the waterfalls". If you are unhappy with sheer drops and are not properly booted, take the advised path. However, unless committed to that option, continue following the narrower paths above the river with dramatic views of the gorge seen intermittently between the tracery of the trees.

Hill walkers will have no difficulty with this path, even so care is required and the path is soon making a way beneath a rock overhang with the river 60 or 70 feet below. Again the rocky table from which the river launches itself into space is seen. A mild scramble will take you down for an eye-level view of the twin falls.

Having inspected and perhaps taken a souvenir photograph of Sgwd Isaf Clun-gwyn, retrace your steps to the path above. Continue with the path which gradually climbs diagonally left to follow a narrow way between bracken, birch and oak, high above the gorge and swinging away from the river. The third waterfall shown on the map Sgwd y Pannwr is off our route.

The path emerges into more open country, where swing left on a clear path. This immediately divides, but take the left fork signed to Sgwd yr

Eira. (Note — ignore the path by the sign which heads back through the woods). Follow the grassy path with the woods to your left and fine views to distant mountains forward half right and the cliffs of the gorge rising above the river on your right.

The path becomes more obvious although narrow and, when a T-junction is met, turn left, uphill on a rocky path. (The right turn will take you down to the riverside and another set of falls but with no convenient exit). A crossing path is soon met with woodland facing you, turn right with this soon with glimpses to the falls ahead.

After a couple of minutes' walking a stile is seen on the wood edge. Turn sharp right here to make a long and steep zig-zag descent to the foot of the gorge aided by steps to go forward to the base of Sgwd yr Eira — Waterfall of the Snow.

A curtain of water cascades down some thirty feet from an overhang so that you may walk behind the fall – dry but deafened by the roar of the tumbling waters – to the opposite bank of the River Hepste. From here, paths climb the ravine leading to the car park at Craig y Ddinas. There are opportunities for linear walks with the aid of two cars, or you could continue to the village of Penderyn for a possible round walk back to Porth yr Ogof. Our route takes a more direct line of return.

What comes down must in this instance go up and the way must be retraced to the top of the gorge. Masochists will count the steps between the puffing and blowing, others may simply acknowledge that it was well worth the effort.

Turn left at the top of the steps, following the broad track with the woodland boundary to your right. Soon the path swings northwards and is followed for about 600 yards. When a path is seen making a short winding descent forward left, take it for another view of the Sgwd Clun-gwyn. Instead of edging along the waterfall as on your outward journey, take the higher route. When the path divides after a short distance, take the left fork, downhill, which quickly returns you to the footbridge. Do not cross but continue upstream to return to the car park in just over three-quarters of a mile.

The Brecon Beacons – Walk Seven: Craig Cerrig-gleisiad and Fan Frynych

Starting Point: Layby/picnic site off the A470.

Access: Six miles south-west of Brecon and one mile north of the Storey Arms car park.

Distance: 7½ miles.

Detail: A scenic route which includes a long stretch of fairly level walking but with an exceptionally steep descent on the return leg. Please see opening paragraphs for a linear alternative.

Map: 1:25,000 Outdoor Leisure Map No. 12.

Nearest Toilets: Pont ar Daf car park 1¼ miles to the south of the starting point.

Sometimes that which we come to admire we may unthinkingly damage or even destroy – witness the scarring of the landscape that is so evident on the better-known areas of the Brecon Beacons. Delicate environments require both care and restraint if they and the plants, birds and animals which they support are to be preserved. The Countryside Council for Wales is dedicated to this work with the establishment of reserves throughout the country, in the interests of scientific study and conservation. This does not mean that the KEEP OUT notices inevitably go up, with the enjoyment of the area limited to the few who have permits. Most reserves are welcoming to visitors prepared to accept minor restrictions, which may include keeping strictly to agreed routes. One such is the 1200 acre Craig Cerrig-gleisiad a Fan Frynych Reserve; this encompasses a dramatic landscape of high cliffs and ravines where arctic alpine plants still survive and high grassy moorland, where keen-eyed predators seek their prey.

Some public rights of way pass through the reserve and, with the advice of the warden, these have been selected to offer a route presenting the landscape to advantage. Additionally, there are several permissive paths within the reserve and these are clearly shown on boards sited at intervals. Recent editions of the O/S Outdoor Leisure Map have added this information, but these routes have not been used in devising the walk which follows since such paths may be subject to closure or diversion. Nevertheless, it may be preferable to adapt the suggested route to take advantage of the permissive paths, the one from the Pont Blaen-cwm-du, for example, or a circuit including Fan Frynych and Craig Cerrig-gleisiad.

As already indicated the return leg of this walk includes some rough ground and an exceptionally steep pathless descent. Much of the scenic pleasure of the walk can be enjoyed from the initially fairly level drove road which passes along the western edges of the reserve. Access to this can be gained by the minor road which heads south-west from the A4215 to Forest Lodge. The old track, which is joined by the Roman road Sarn Helen, runs for five miles to a minor road near Fan Nedd. A "there and back" expedition from Forest Lodge to Pont Blaen-cwm-du will total five miles. A longer excursion might be considered together with a visit to the Brecon Beacons Mountain Centre, north-west of Libanus, where there are parking, picnic, information and toilet facilities.

The Walk

Few walkers are likely to be encountered during this circuit and your only companions may prove to be white-rumped wheatears, smooth gliding ravens or a sharp-eyed hovering kestrel.

From the layby on the A470 cross the stile by the metal gateway and go forward. Immediately to your right is a plaque commemorating "Eric Bartlett 1920-1986 who did so much for wild life and the countryside". The boundary of the reserve is reached in 300 yards with the dramatic nature of the landscape immediately apparent.

The circlet of Craig Cerrig-gleisiad falls in a craggy turmoil from its highest point of 2034 ft. Often dark and forbidding, earlier travel writers might well have described them as awesome cliffs. The morning sun strikes one face of the crags with a glancing light, leaving the northern rocks in the deepest shadow. By evening all is a sombre darkness and the patient, and perhaps lucky, photographer may be rewarded with a fiery sunset against the blackest of mountain silhouettes.

Immediately beyond the gate swing right travelling north on a clear rising path which, for the first three-quarters of a mile, is never far from the stone wall seen to your right. To the east the twin peaks of the Beacons, Corn

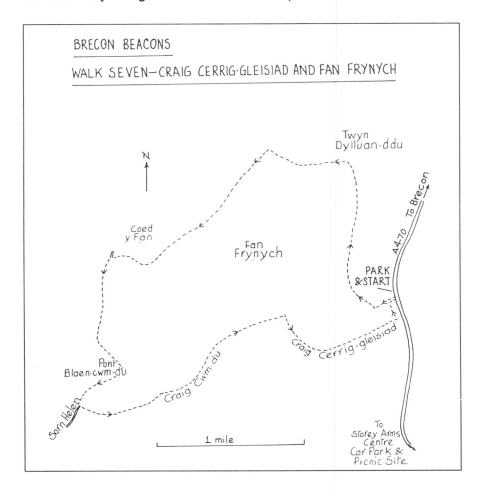

BRECON BEACONS

WALK SEVEN—CRAIG CERRIG-GLEISIAD AND FAN FRYNYCH

Du and Pen y Fan thrust their sharp northern faces above the great bank that climbs to the 2030 ft summit of Y Gyrn. Fan Frynych, (2034 ft) on your left is by-passed as the path heads towards the lesser height of Twyn Dyllaun-ddu. Although at times narrow, the path is clear throughout, passing through bracken or heather and stunted gorse.

Just short of Twyn Dylluan-ddu, pass through a gateway and take the broad falling track which heads west to a further gate in 700 yards, where the reserve is temporarily deserted. Continue with the track which now swings to the north-west for 300 yards to an old drove road. Here turn left and follow it for two and a half miles.

The track is wide and clear and for most of the way pursues a fairly level but highly scenic course on the western edges of the reserve. At this point the Roman Road, Sarn Helen, will be noted as a dotted line on the map about three-quarters of a mile to the west, which eventually joins our track.

Few directions are needed and the walker can safely admire the superb scenery. This is, at first, concentrated on the left where sheep pasture steepens to crags surmounted by the 2063 ft Fan Frynych. In half a mile the larch plantation of Coed y Fan is passed to your right and the reserve re-entered.

About 300 yards beyond the plantation, the track divides. Ignore the diagonal left fork guarded by a gate and continue with the fence line and hawthorn to your right. The track curves with the contour and is joined by a road coming in from the right — the junction with the Sarn Helen. The direction has now swung to the south giving views over the valley of the Afon Senni to Fan Bwlch Chwyth and its disused quarry. Ahead is the 2175 ft summit of Fan Nedd over which permissive paths run through the Fforest Fawr — The Great Forest of Brecknock. The summits to our left form part of the eastern boundary of the forest. A brief change of direction, to the south-east, provides a superb prospect of the double elipse of Craig Cwm Du, a long towering craggy mountain wall. This old road through the hills offers an almost unmatched spectacle and there is more to come as the path dips down to cross the stream at Pont Blaen-cwm-du.

Here there is a long view up the cwm as the crags to the south and the slopes of Fan Frynych close in. To see it at its best, walk downstream a few yards so that your perspective has the little bridge in the foreground and the valley held in the vice formed by the soaring hills and cliffs. On a fine day, there are many photographic opportunities with foregrounds brightened by patches of heather and stunted gorse as the eye is led deep into the heart of the hills. A place that will be long remembered.

From the bridge, continue with the road as it climbs for nearly half a mile to the south-western boundary of the reserve, signalled by an information board at the gate. Here is another good viewpoint, this time to look down the long valley of the Afon Senni where six miles to the north the river joins the Usk at Sennybridge.

Now the pleasures so far enjoyed have to be paid for with some rougher walking, a steep ascent and an even sharper descent. The directions can be shortened to a single sentence: beyond the gate turn left and follow the fence line over the hills until the wood by the A470 is reached where turn left to return to the picnic site.

Rather more flesh is required to clothe the bare bones of these directions, to which is added a suggestion for an alternative path.

The return, which runs close to the edge of Craig Cwm-du, begins with a sharp ascent over grassy slopes, a climb of 560 feet in about 500 yards, keeping the fence to your left throughout the return. Despite several changes of angle, it follows the contours of the scarp edges. The general direction is north of east, sometimes with a path to be found a few yards from the fence. The ascent is broken by a small maze of sheep pens which can be negotiated by a series of gates if unoccupied or skirted round if in use.

The western arc includes Fan Nedd and as height is gained a distant grey profile of the Black Mountain. As the way levels out there are views deep into the cwm with the tiny silver thread of the stream and the road winding along the flanks of the hills. A distant forward view to the Beacons is soon lost and the land falls away into an area of soft rush, always an indicator of damp ground and in a wet season a detour round the edge may be advisable.

The higher ground is soon regained and a view of the Beacons—Corn Du and Pen y Fan and their long buttressing ridges riding up from the north. The various angles of the fence line will ultimately bring you to a boundary fence running north/south with a stile and a Reserve information board. A permissive path (indicated as requiring special care) runs south and east along the scarp edge of Craig Cerrig-gleisiad and for the most part only a few feet away from the route described in these pages—if this path is still operational, you may opt to use it as an alternative route.

Crossing Pont Blaen-cwm-du with the cliffs of Craig Cwm-du behind

Our way continues on the outside of the fence, a route which has some safety considerations in bad weather. From the notice board turn sharp right, (south) along the fence climbing to reach the highest point of the walk, 2063 ft. As you top the rise the path swings to the left with a view of the sharp cliff face. An initial steady descent provides views to the Beacons, and of the sheep and hill ponies who share the grazing on the slopes of Gorilw. Far below to your left the dry stone wall which was followed in the opening stages of the walk snakes over the hillside.

The descent sharpens to an uncomfortable angle which eventually brings you to a gate by the small wood at the foot of the slope. Once through the gate turn left and in 200 yards, as a stream is reached, swing right to the picnic site and layby.

The Brecon Beacons — Walk Eight: Carn Pica — Waun Rydd and the Canal

Starting Point: The Welsh Water Company's car park north of the Talybont Reservoir.

Access: Leave the A40 by the minor road signed south-west of Talybont-on-Usk. At a T-junction turn right (signed Pencelli), and in a quarter of a mile turn left — signed to Torpantau — to cross the canal by the lift bridge. Take the road through Aber to reach the car park found on the left in a mile and a quarter.

Distance: 10½ miles

Detail: A steep ascent to Carn Pica to cross the Waun Rydd plateau. A long and easy descent leads to Pencelli and on to a return by the canal tow-path. Boots and a clear day to assist wayfinding over the plateau are essential — some widely spaced cairns mark the way.

Map: 1:25,000 Outdoor Leisure Map No. 12 and edge of 13.

Toilets: At car park.

This walk, which includes a steep ascent and crossing of a moorland plateau, is different in character from the paths explored in the central Beacons. The route should be reserved until acquaintance has been made with the main peaks which, from this approach, present sudden and dramatic profiles as the walk progresses. Wide views to the Black Mountains appear and disappear at intervals. In places the paths are narrow and less distinct than those encountered in the Pen y Fan area. Unless there has been a long period of dry weather, some soggy sections will have to be negotiated.

There is a small information centre at the car park with a display illustrating the changes wrought upon the landscape by the demands for water. Prior permission is required from the nearby Filter House to use the small and pleasant camp site.

The Walk

From the car park return to the road and turn right towards Aber. In 300 yards take the metalled lane on the left.

Immediately on the right an old stone wall plays host to wall pennywort. The verges provide an unofficial nature reserve with a wild flower garden that includes herb robert, digitalis, meadowsweet and speedwell with honeysuckle festooning the hedges.

The lane bends to the south-west and in 400 yards turns sharp right where it is signed "Private Road Ahead". At this point the road should be abandoned in favour of a wide grassy way-marked track beyond a gate. In 200 yards ignore the stile seen directly ahead and bear right with the track to continue to a further gateway with a tiny stream to your right.

Just beyond the gate a small tributary stream is crossed but your generally westward direction is maintained as indeed it is for the next three miles. The way continues on a grassy track which becomes more open as it steepens. A narrow but obvious path to your right crosses the stream, beyond which there is a good view to the lower Talybont Valley — in high summer a very green and pleasant land. Continue uphill keeping the forest boundary to your right. Soon a gateway and stile is encountered beyond which lies the open hillside. Continue ignoring the track which edges off half left.

The long pull out of the valley is rewarded with improving views of forest, moorland and mountain. A backward look will reveal the distinctive outline of the Table Mountain above Crickhowell and the long ridge which runs northwards over Pen Cerrig-calch. The shapely Sugar Loaf above Abergavenny is easily identified. Near to hand the no less comely Tor y Foel rises to 1807 feet above the Talybont Reservoir with its upper 500 feet clear of the forest.

The woodland on your right thins out and the stone wall turns sharply to the north. Continue forward on a clear track over a hillside clothed in bracken, grass and bilberry with the ubiquitous sinister carrion crow dressed in his undertaker's black. By the time the first cairn is reached the views have widened further with a greater expanse of the forest now unveiled. This is too well ordered to be solely the work of nature whose seemingly haphazard planting is so often the more appealing. Now the first summit, Twyn Du, comes into view, the narrowing path passes along its southern flank, well below the 1750 ft summit providing a stretch of almost level walking.

The view ahead is to the long green cliff of Craig y Fan with the cairn at its northern end, on Carn Pica, indicating your direction of travel. The path curves very slightly to the right with a short soggy section to be crossed before the steep climb to Carn Pica begins. The upper slopes are hard work with some erosion apparent and seemingly getting worse.

The cairn is not your usual careless tumble of stones but a ten-feet elongated beehive carefully constructed in reddy-brown rock. It does service as a landmark, a welcome resting place and a splendid viewpoint from which the concentration is on the eastern arc. Llangorse Lake, sparkling or not, attracts attention, five miles distant with its armada of small sailing boats visible as white dots upon the black water. The Sugar Loaf offers itself for admiration once more. Crickhowell's Table Mountain with the long ridges of the Black Mountains are presented to perfection. To the right the limestone quarry faces will be noted beyond the Talybont Forest with a succession of blue grey hills ranged along the southern limits of the horizon. To the north a farming landscape is announced by the patterning of the enclosures, multicoloured in green, brown and yellow.

From Carn Pica the route continues with a gentle increase in height, still westwards but curving a little to the north as the grassy plateau is traversed — a sometimes soggy but (in clear weather) not difficult passage of just under a mile. After only a few steps the summits of the central Beacons appear dramatically ahead. Less startling is the next cairn, modest in proportions but still a welcome marker.

The track from the cairn is narrow but after passing two pools set close together on Waun Rydd becomes more distinct — for a while. The long cliff of Graig Fan Ddu which was followed in Walk Five impresses, as do the sphinx-like outlines of the Beacons. The erosion of the peaty terrain is more evident and you will be obliged to pick a way across deep black troughs. The crossing of the plateau, over 2500 ft at its highest point, brings the walker to a cross-roads of paths.

To the west lies the route above the deep northern cwms via Fan y Big to Cribyn, Pen y Fan and Corn Ddu. To the south, the long traverse of the scarp edge of Craig y Fan ddu and the western end of the Talybont Forest, routes already explored in earlier walks.

Now our way turns north-eastwards following Rhiw Bwlch y Ddwyallt, above Cwm Cwareli.

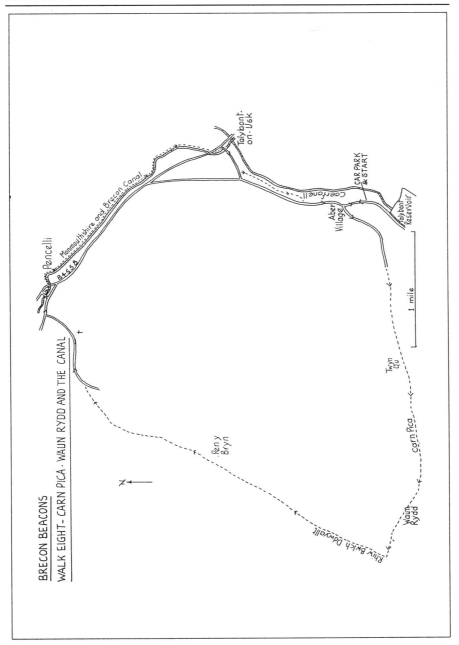

BRECON BEACONS
WALK EIGHT – CARN PICA · WAUN RYDD AND THE CANAL

Hill ponies may be encountered grazing along the ridge. Sheep, at their whitest in July after shearing, dot the rough pastures between the ridges and swifts in perpetual motion dive and swoop for insects far below.

There is a long steady and satisfying descent in an almost straight line for the next two and a half miles. When a path heads off diagonally right, ignore it and keep to the main path. As you round the hill which has blocked the view to your right Llangorse Lake reappears and again there are views to the Black Mountains. When the path divides at a Y-junction, take the right fork heading east of north. A sideways glance to the right reveals the handsome cairn of Carn Pica with Craig Pwllfa falling sharply to the north-east. There are fine backward views to the sharp edged Beacons perhaps glowering darkly under their misty crown of clouds

The Black Mountains temporarily disappear from sight as you pass along the western flanks of the 1843 ft summit of Pen y Bryn. As height is lost the rough grass gives way to bracken and a stream (which falls to Coed Tyle-du) is crossed by a rowan tree. The path divides just a step or two before the tree is reached, take the right fork, passing the tree on your left. The path falls wide and clear through the bracken with a stone wall seen

Carn Pica and the view to the Black Mountains

to your left. As the stone wall runs away from you, keep to the grassy path and head to the right in the general direction of Llangorse Lake. Descend with a distant church seen forward half left and with a fence about 60 yards to your right.

The slope steepens, the strip of bracken narrows and fence lines converge to a gateway and stile. Nettles and gnarled hawthorn have taken command of an old hollow way, so follow the field edge until a stile returns you to the path. This leads to a minor road through a guard of honour of hawthorn, birch and hazel.

Turn left down the lane, its hedges thick with honeysuckle, the promise of hazel nuts to come in the autumn and with a fine prospect of the successive profiles of the Black Mountains. The lane is followed for three-quarters of a mile, passing Llanfegian church, seemingly in grave danger of being overcome by an advancing wilderness.

On reaching a road junction turn right, passing Pencelli Court Farm with its ancient stone barns now roofed in more prosaic fashion. Soon, the Monmouthshire and Brecon Canal is reached. Turn left over the bridge, which strangely carries a metal plaque bearing instructions from the Great Western Railway to drivers of locomotives and others. A sign of the decline of the canal and its acquisition by its more modern rival. Once over the bridge, turn right to join the canal tow-path which is followed south-eastwards for two miles.

A pleasant way, fringed with meadowsweet, cranesbill, forget-me-not, rosebay willow herb, clumps of water iris and shaded by beech, ash, sycamore and oak. A succession of arched stone bridges and iron drawbridges punctuate the way – crossings to accommodate the movement of livestock and tractors.

The end of the tow-path trail is signalled by the white painted drawbridge at Talybont. The return to the car park, a mile and a quarter to the south, can be effected directly by road; as this can be busy on summer weekends, a partial route by field paths is suggested as an alternative.

Turn along the road to Aber and, soon after passing the Wilson School Field Studies Centre, take the footpath on the left over a stone stile. Head diagonally right over the field to a further stile. Follow the course of the Caerfanell upstream until the path turns left over a footbridge. Do not cross the bridge but go forward for a few yards to a stile and then turn right up the fence line to the road by Aber Farm. Turn left to return to your starting point which is reached in just under half a mile.

The Usk Valley

The Usk Valley makes both a division and a link. A division since it effectively separates the Beacons from the Black Mountains, and a link along riverside paths and canal tow-path to Abergavenny and the Black Mountains.

The River Usk rises on Waun Lwyd beneath the long northern shadows of the Black Mountain peaks on the boundary of Powys and Dyfed. Quickly strengthened by the contributions of a score of streams, its progress is soon arrested as its resources are tapped to fill the Usk Reservoir. Three miles on it reaches Trecastle, where a motte and bailey guarded the east-west way through the mountains. This is now the route of the A40 with which it keeps close company for the next 36 miles. A far cry from the busy highway that roars out of London, for now it has been tamed and, between Abergavenny and Brecon, it provides an enjoyable scenic route with especially fine views of the Beacons. At Crickhowell the road has narrowed to such an extent that lorries are hard put to pass each other.

The Usk has long been valued for its fishing – salmon and trout are a particular feature. Writing in the late twelfth century Gerald of Wales mentions both and comments that the Wye is better provided with salmon and the Usk better stocked with trout. There is no continuous public right of way along the banks of the Usk, but intermittent paths offer enjoyable walks.

The growing needs of industry in the eighteenth century saw the often shallow Usk being joined by another waterway – now known as the Monmouthshire and Brecon Canal, with the tow-path providing a through route for the long distance walker.

Fine views over the Usk Valley can be enjoyed from a succession of high points including Tor y Foel, Blorenge and the Sugar Loaf. River and canalside paths allow a closer acquaintance which can be extended beyond the three suggested walks that sample the cool and shady paths between Brecon and Crickhowell. Points of interest include the Brynich Aqueduct, the flight of five locks to the west of Llangynird and the Ashford Tunnel.

Further details and a descriptive leaflet useful to both walkers and boating enthusiasts are available from British Waterways, the Wharf, Govilon, Abergavenny NP7 9NY.

The ancient Usk Bridge, Crickhowell

The Usk Valley – Walk One:
Tor y Foel and the Canal

Starting Point: Welsh Water Company's car park north of the Talybont Dam.

Access: Leave the A40 by the minor road south-west to Talybont-on-Usk. At a T-junction turn right signed Pencelli, in a quarter of a mile turn left (signed to Torpantau) and cross the canal by the lift bridge. Take the road through Aber to reach the car park on the left in a mile and a quarter.

Distance: 9½ miles.

Detail: Ascent through woodland continues to Tor y Foel, then a long falling ridge leads on to a return by the Monmouthshire and Brecon Canal and woodland.

Maps: 1:25,000 Outdoor Leisure Map 13.

Toilets: At car park.

This is a walk for one of those hazy days when the views from the topmost peaks may be restricted to a mile or two rather than far distant horizons. Several elements combine to provide a satisfying circuit of lake, forest, high open country and shaded tow-path.

The Walk

From the car park return towards the road but take the metalled drive signed "Filter House and reservoir only". When this divides curve left to pass the Talybont Water Treatment Plant with the green slopes of the dam seen ahead. Cross the foot-bridge by the outlet – the Afon Caerfanell which having been detained in its progress down the valley is released in a great spurting gush to resume its short journey to join the River Usk.

Once over the bridge, head half left up the slope on a wide grassy track which soon becomes a hollow way. At the top of the lane pass through a gateway and turn right on a track which intersects with a disused railway line. Follow the footpath signed on the left and continue forward on the track now with good views of the valley, which improve as you reach the eastern end of the dam.

Cross the cattle grid by the sign to the study centre and go ahead to the metalled road which runs along the eastern slopes of the reservoir. (Note: there is no public access to the waterside).

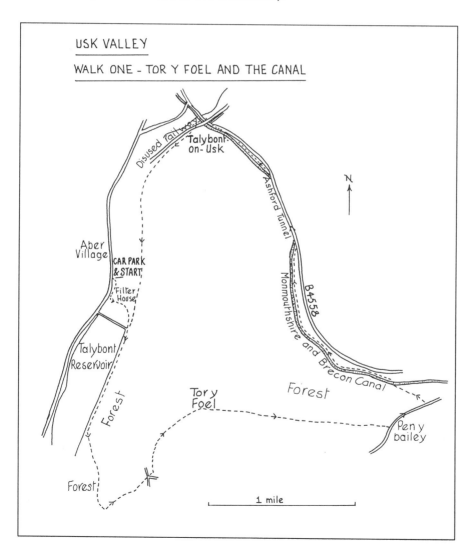

USK VALLEY

WALK ONE - TOR Y FOEL AND THE CANAL

Construction of the reservoir began in 1932 and took seven years. It is two and a quarter miles long and has blended into the landscape so well that, once out of sight of the dam and the treatment buildings, it is easy to fall into the habit of calling it a lake – a much prettier word than reservoir. Certainly it presents an attractive scene, fringed by the forest and backed by high hills.

Clumps of rhododendron border the reservoir and, in summer, meadowsweet is thickly clustered to your left. Across the water, Allt Lwyd rises above the forest to its 2145 ft summit and on to the saddle which makes the connection with Craig y Fan. Carn Pica at the northern end of the scarp displays the small but sharply-outlined beehive of its cairn. Meadowsweet gives way to banks of rosebay willow herb – ablaze in July fully justifying its common name – fireweed. The wooded fringes of the lake provide a sheltered habitat for birds and buzzards may be seen at close range. Winter sees an increase in the numbers of wildfowl on the lake.

After a while the metalled lane becomes a stony track climbing steadily above the lake. About three-quarters of a mile after joining the lake edge, a sharp left turn takes the track under the bridge that once carried the railway. In its day this must have been an enjoyably scenic route.

The old line can be traced on the map for much of its course as it runs through the forest and close to three reservoirs to Pontsticill and on towards Merthyr Tydfil. Just beyond the bridge there is a good viewpoint and you may hear the chimes of a distant ice cream van as it makes the rounds of the car parks along the Talybont Valley. The purple spiky flower you may see along the way is selfheal which was reputed to be beneficial in the treatment of throat and other infections.

Continue climbing up the rough track and ignore the first left turn. As height is gained the southern end of the lake comes into view. After a while the forest road takes a sharp turn to the left. In a few yards, turn sharp right with more open woodland to your right and, on the left, closely regimented larches stand shoulder to shoulder in stout defence of the hillside. When a (slight) diagonal crossing path is met, turn left with a steep pull to a broad crossing track. Go over this and head uphill for about 100 yards to reach a small gate leading on to the open hillside. The gate, which currently is showing signs of its age, is wired up and must be treated as a stile. Take the path which runs through bracken roughly north of east with the summit of Tor y Foel seen ahead.

A short wet patch has to be crossed where water leaches out of the hillside but the path improves as it passes through bracken. As it draws level with the edge of the forest it curves to a narrow road by the gate that guards the bridleway to Bwlch-y-Waun.

Take the path which climbs, northwards at first, to Tor y Foel. The higher ground fills in more detail of the curving loop of the forest surrounding the lake. A wide clear grassy path through bilberry brings you to the first false summit, before swinging to the north-east to the top of the hill which finally peaks at 1807 ft.

The cairn is a very modest affair and much of the lower valley has disappeared. To take in the view more fully you must go forward a few paces to the edge of the little plateau. Below lie the houses and farms of the Talybont Valley, with the dam holding back the impounded waters gathered from the hills by scores of streams. The westward outlook is to the eastern end of the Beacons range, and over the valley to Allt Lwyd, Twyn Du and Carn Pica. Immediately to the north is the Janus-like hill forested on one face and farmed on the other. The 1268-foot summit is crowned with a hill fort, with the remains of a settlement on its southern slopes. In summer swallows swoop low over Tor y Foel gathering in the bountiful harvest of insects to feed their ever hungry broods and flocks of jackdaws scavenge across the tops – beware the smaller bird who leaves her nest unprotected!

From the mini cairn, walk eastwards over the short plateau and onto a lesser summit. There is now a steady descent of nearly a mile, with the bilberry and grass giving way to bracken as height is lost. Llangorse Lake will be seen five miles to the north and forward the views are down the valley of the Usk to the Black Mountains. As height is lost, the path follows the outside edge of a forest with a stone wall on your left. A fence closing in from the right funnels the path towards a gateway, beyond which it runs as a hollow way, passing an ancient blue birch so decrepit that surely it cannot stand here much longer. The descent continues beyond a further gateway to reach the road by Pen-y-bailey farm. Turn left and follow the lane.

Wild flowers abound on the steep banks of the hedgerows including tufted vetch, cousin of the garden sweet pea. Wild strawberry and hazel nuts may provide unexpected refreshment at the appropriate seasons. The villages of the vale are seen ahead with the wooded Myarth Hill beyond which looms the Pen Cerrig-calch ridge above Crickhowell which peaks on Pen Allt-mawr at 2359 ft.

In a little over a quarter of a mile, abandon the lane to take the path on the left opposite to where a track joins the lane from the right. There are two gates here; take the left-hand one and head diagonally left on a falling track towards a clump of trees with the canal seen to your right. Continue for 100 yards beyond the next gateway, passing a long white house on your right to emerge on to a lane by the canal. Cross the bridge and turn left over a stone stile, descending steps to the tow-path which is now pursued westwards for two and a quarter miles.

A pleasant shaded passage punctuated by a series of little arched bridges. A myriad reflections dance upon the water. Wild flowers line the way, digitalis, meadowsweet, pink campion and a tangle of brambles which threaten to completely overwhelm the hedgerow. Summertime entertainment may be provided by a convoy of young ducklings possessed of energy beyond their tender age as they battle against the wake of narrow boats whose junior crew throw bread to them.

In a mile and a quarter, the Ashford Tunnel is reached, a narrow black hole with the faintest suggestion of distant light. Here the cruising narrow boats disappear underground and the walker must take to the road for 400 yards. What happens, you may wonder, if one narrow boat meets another making its way in the inky darkness from the opposite direction … an inland waterways version of a Mexican standoff perhaps?

The canal emerges from the darkness by Ashford House and the grassy verge between it and the road is followed until the tow-path proper can be rejoined. The Travellers Rest Inn is seen in half a mile. Pass under the old railway bridge, beyond which lies canal bridge number 143 behind the White Hart Inn at Talybont. Now leave the tow-path and cross the bridge, taking the track which bears to the right.

In 200 yards the track which crosses the former railway bridge still displaying its 24 ton weight limit, and bear right. The way emerges from a long rising green tunnel to give views to the hills. Buzzards may again be seen or their mewing cry heard. Continue beyond a five barred gate with a forest road coming in from diagonal left. Forsake the rising path to follow the broader forest road which is edged with Aarons Rod. The road falls steadily and is joined by a path coming in from diagonal right.

Ashford Tunnel

Maintain your forward (southern) direction until you reach the dam, about a mile and a half after leaving the canal. You may now retrace your steps through the waterworks area to return to the car park. Alternatively cross the dam which provides good views and the possibility that an ice cream van may be parked on the western bank of the reservoir.

Once over the dam turn right and follow the road for a quarter of a mile to return to the car park.

The Usk Valley – Walk Two: Tor y Foel

Starting Point: Foot of Tor y Foel – above the Talybont Forest.

Access: From the A40 take the Talybont-on-Usk road and at the T-junction turn left. In 300 yards turn right on the No Through Road which is followed for 2½ miles. When the open area above the forest is reached there is space to leave cars near the foot of Tor y Foel.

Distance: 3½ miles.

Detail: A shortened version of Usk Valley Walk One. Outward leg by old bridleway with steady climb to return over Tor y Foel giving good views over the Usk and the Talybont Valleys.

Maps: 1:25,000 Outdoor Leisure Map 13

This walk provides a short but worthwhile excursion suitable for a summer's afternoon or a short winter's day with easy wayfinding.

The Walk

From the open area of grass and bracken above the forest there is a view over the trees to the Talybont Reservoir and the eastern end of the Brecon Beacons.

Take the gated bridleway by the stone wall with the sign that announces Bwlch-y-Waun. Follow the metalled track eastwards with the steep slopes of Tor y Foel to your left. In just under half a mile Bwlch-y-Waun Farm is reached. The track passes between the farm house and its ancillary buildings and continues as a grassy track along the flanks of the hillside.

This old country way is lined by gnarled hawthorn, ancient beech and, later, hazel. These trees were originally layered to form part of a hedge but in places only the hazel remains, now left to its own devices.

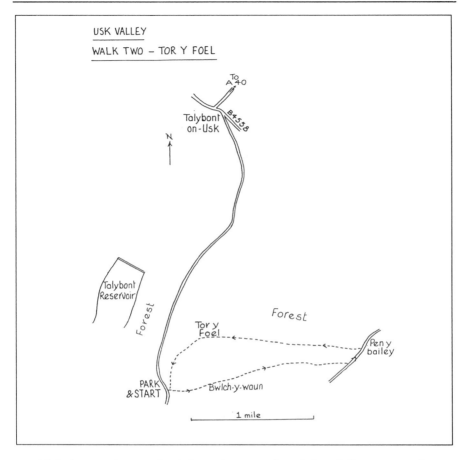

USK VALLEY

WALK TWO – TOR Y FOEL

To A 40

Talybont on-Usk

B4558

N

Talybont Reservoir

Forest

Forest

Tor y Foel

Pen y bailey

PARK & START

Bwlch-y-waun

1 mile

This is a quiet track giving views to the right of the remote farming valley of the Afon Crawnon sheltered by the hills which quickly rise to the limestone plateau of Mynydd Llangynidr. Shake holes dot the map and a cave, Ogof Fawr, is now noted for the shelter it gave to the Chartists during the unrest of the 1840s. There were particularly violent incidents in Newport in November 1839. The towns former mayor, John Frost, led a rebellion in support of the movement, but there was heavy loss of life when troops opened fire. He and others were tried and condemned to death at the Monmouth assizes, but the sentence was reduced to transportation.

In a little under a mile, there is a stone barn on your right. Beyond the buildings two gates face you. Do not be tempted by the obvious track which rises beyond the left-hand gate but continue on through the other gate, maintaining your easterly direction with the track less obvious at first. It soon re-appears with more hazel and is lined here by sturdy oaks and the ubiquitous hawthorn – a favoured plant of the hedge maker; millions must have been planted during the wholesale enclosures of fields during the eighteenth century. Hazel was extremely useful to the countryman: it was coppiced to provide wood for hurdles, pegs for thatchers, and it was used by water diviners; it also provided kindling wood, and cob nuts in September.

Three hundred yards from the barn, the track joins a narrow lane. Turn left here and climb to reach Pen-y-bailey Farm in a further 300 yards. Now turn immediately left to take the track beyond a wooden gate. Almost a twin to the one which has just been left, it climbs steadily in a hollow way for a quarter of a mile or so to reach a gate which leads to the open hillside.

Beyond the gate, maintain your westerly direction on a clear path which climbs at first through bracken and bilberry to reach the 1897 ft summit plateau of Tor y Foel in a mile. The climb provides retrospective views down the Usk Valley towards Crickhowell with Table Mountain in view and the great grey bulk of the westernmost ridge of the Black Mountains. To your right the silvered River Usk will be seen following a straightish northerly course. The rim of the plateau offers an excellent prospect of the Talybont Valley, almost the full two-mile length of the reservoir and, beyond the forest, the westerly arc of Allt Lwyd, Craig y Fan and Carn Pica.

The track changes direction from the summit swinging south-west, then south to make a half mile return on a clear falling path to your starting point.

One misty day, I passed a pair of racing pigeons perched on a small rock surveying the landscape from the slopes of Tor y Foel. The pair were in first class condition, in no way distressed, and I assume that they had paused here to get their bearings. Maybe the temporary absence of the sun and the reduction in visibility of familiar landmarks interrupted their scheduled flight.

The Usk Valley – Walk Three: Llangynidr and the River Usk

Starting Point: Llangynidr car park north of the village

Access: By the B4558 4 miles west of Crickhowell – or 3 miles east of Talybont-on-Usk.

Distance: 3 miles.

Detail: A mainly level walk – out by the canal, return by the river – some rough ground.

Map: 1:25,000 Outdoor Leisure Map No 13.

Toilets: Opposite car park.

This short walk is what Sir Thomas Beecham, in quite another context, used to call a lollipop, for it follows a delightfully wild stretch of the River Usk. The contrast with the tamed waters of the canal could scarcely be more dramatically illustrated.

The Walk

From the car park, turn left, (west) following the road for 200 yards to Waterloo House, now housing a cycle frame specialist. Turn right over a stile found opposite and follow the field boundary with the hedge on your left. At the bottom of the field, cross a trickle of a stream. Turn left through a gateway then immediately right over a stile which in summer is festooned with wild hops. A canal bridge is now seen ahead, make for this and once over the bridge turn left to cross a stone stile to join the tow-path.

Turn left under the bridge (No. 130) and follow the path eastwards. (Note all the canal bridges are numbered in descending order on their eastern faces).

The tow-path is now followed for nearly a mile, a quiet shady way with Ta-

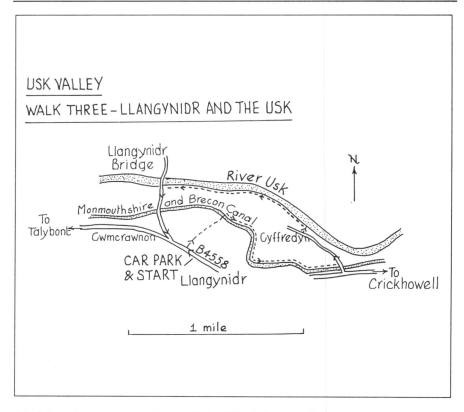

USK VALLEY

WALK THREE – LLANGYNIDR AND THE USK

ble Mountain and a snippet of the Black Mountains seen ahead. Black-berries and cob nuts in the hedgerow may provide a small buffet in late summer. The mauve flower which may be noted along the water's edge is water mint.

When bridge 126 is reached, leave the tow-path, climbing the bank to turn left along the narrow Cyffredyn Lane. (The roadside face of the bridge is host to ivy-leafed toadflax with its tiny blue orchid-like flowers). This quiet twisting by-way is pursued for just over a quarter of a mile to the riverside hamlet. A series of cottages is passed – Glandwr, Cyffredyn and finally Usk Cottage – the first in a small row. Just beyond this point take the wide path on the right which runs between stone walls and leads to the river bank. Turn left upstream to follow the river as far as the six-arched, four-hundred year old Llangynidr Bridge, which is reached in a little under a mile.

The River Usk and Tor y Foel from the ancient Llangnidr bridge

This is a delightfully wild stretch of the river, flowing fast and free, clear and sparkling, in continuous voice, tinkling over stones, roaring over rocks, as it falls down the valley between tree-lined and sometimes cliff-like banks. Patches of Indian balsam lend a slightly tropical atmosphere to the scene, ducks battle their watery way between boulders or, startled, take flight in noisy commotion. A heron rises from its fishing in a slow lugubrious flight with legs trailing.

The path, sometimes close to the water's edge where you may linger upon a great flat pavement of almost level rock when the river is low, or climbing between a wire fence and a 60-foot drop to the swirling waters.

Half a mile from Cyffredyn the waterfall promised to students of the map is reached. A modest affair as waterfalls go, dropping only a few feet, but with energy, enthusiasm and a satisfying roar. Above the fall, a large rocky outcrop shaded by overhanging oaks allows the walker to pause and watch the turmoil of the river as it curves in a rush of white water and throws itself upon the rocks.

When the bridge is reached, leave the path and turn left towards Llangynidr. But, before doing so, take a stroll across the ancient bridge from which the river can again be enjoyed. Peer down to see what lurks in the still pools below or watch the tumbling dash of the river, fearful of being late for its appointed meeting with the Severn estuary at Newport. Upstream the shaded river's course is looked over by the 1806 ft summit of Tor y Foel.

Returning from the bridge, the road climbs to cross the canal and then on to the Cwmcrawnon Road, where you turn left, signed Crickhowell, to return to your starting point.

Abergavenny

Abergavenny, so often described as the Gateway to Wales, makes an excellent base for exploring the Usk Valley and the rewarding but not over demanding hills which surround the town. Cliche it may now be but Gateway to Wales is very apt. In spring, the traveller heading for the town along the A465 from Hereford finds a ready welcome as he crosses the River Monnow for he is greeted with flowers – not a token gesture but tens of thousands of daffodils which edge the road for several miles.

Abergavenny has for centuries been a busy market town and it still is – as any motorist trying to find a parking space on the Tuesday market day will tell you. Comfortably sited in the valley of the River Usk, Abergavenny provided a home for pre-historic man and later a Roman fort. But it was the Norman conquest that was to start the development of the town around the castle, built in 1090 by Hamelin de Ballon. Initially a timber construction, it was to have a long and turbulent history which continued to the Civil War when it was last garrisoned by supporters of Charles I. The local museum is housed in a former hunting lodge within the castle grounds.

The Parish Church

St Mary's parish church also owes its origins to de Ballon for it was he who founded a Benedictine Priory which, after the dissolution in 1543, survived to serve the town. The church is particularly rich in monuments, some unique. Among the many features of interest is the Herbert Chapel with the tomb of Sir Richard Herbert, a supporter of the Yorkist Edward IV during the Wars of the Roses. During the conflict he was captured at the Battle of Edgcote in July 1469 and beheaded the following day at Banbury. The remains of a Jesse tree are kept in the church, not as so often depicted in a stained glass window, but a substantial wooden carving which once formed part of the reredos.

Nearby, a woman unusually takes on a knightly pose. She was Eva de Cantalupe who became Baroness of Abergavenny in her own right following the death of her husband in 1254; her tomb depicts her with a large shield. The monument to her son, George de Cantalupe, Lord of Abergavenny is one of the church's many treasures. It is a beautifully executed wooden carving, reputed to have been made before his death. It now bears the marks of past vandalism with the head of his faithful hound, which rested at his feet, missing. His master has also suffered, his hands joined in prayer has one arm severed at the wrist.

The carved choir stalls, with their misericord seats date from 1587, but with clear evidence of later unauthorised embellishments. This part of the church did duty as a school in the days when a pen knife was an essential tool for every school boy who used it to sharpen his quill. Evidence is found in the carving on the backs of the benches. Thomas Legge left his mark in 1767, as did the more discreet IR in 1807 whilst the benches themselves are full of the names of pupils who at least demonstrated their ability to write their names neatly.

A further monument is to Dr. David Lewis, who determined not to be forgotten, arranged his own inscription – "Judge of the High Court of Admiralty in the reign of Elizabeth and first principal of Jesus College Oxford, Fellow of All Souls and Principal of New Inn".

The font, which is in part Norman, was lost for a time, but recovered from the churchyard. It still bears the marks of locks which once secured the cover – perhaps a relic of the days when it was necessary to protect holy water from theft by practitioners of witchcraft. Within the church is a bell dated 1408 which carries the inscription "May the bell of John last many years" – this may have saved it from being melted down with its fellows when the peal was recast in 1948.

William de Braose

There is one incident that should be related, for not all the waters of the Usk that have flowed these last eight hundred years can wash

Abergavenny Castle

clean the stain. The year is 1176 and William de Braose, a rich and powerful Lord of the Marches, is master of Abergavenny Castle. It is Christmas, a time of peace and goodwill to all men. It was in that spirit that scores of leaders of the Welsh community, so long in conflict with the Normans, accepted de Braose's invitation to a great feast at the castle. Hardly had they been seated at the table when, at a signal from their host, his men fell upon the guests and savagely slaughtered them. This treachery was without equal even in the annals of the troubled border counties of England and Wales.

No doubt de Braose reasoned in this cruel madness that, in rendering the Welsh leaderless, he was striking a blow that would forever force the native population into submission. Greater men than he have made the same mistake and the years of oppression and attrition were to continue into the succeeding centuries.

Abergavenny – Walk One: Blorenge and the Punchbowl

Starting Point: The Foxhunter car park on the southern flank of the mountain.

Access: From the A465 which passes south of Abergavenny, take the road signed to Llanfoist and Blaenavon, the B4246, and follow this for four miles – a scenic route which climbs steeply along the western slopes of Blorenge. Turn left along the minor road to reach the car park opposite the wireless masts.

Distance: 7 miles. A shorter circuit is given in Walk Two.

Detail: An easy ascent to the summit followed by a rewarding walk which terraces the hillside with excellent views and varied scenery.

Map: Outdoor Leisure Map 13.

Looking south-west from the mound of Abergavenny Castle, the view is blocked by the great bulk of the 1840 ft Blorenge, with access from the north clearly involving a steep but worthwhile climb from the valley of the Usk. The two suggested routes reduce the hard work while in no way detracting from the pleasure of the mountain. The walks can be enjoyed at any time of the year but spring, late May for preference, offers some extras.

Blorenge is a wild rocky moorland covered in tufted grass, heather, bilberry and in summer the wispy heads of cotton grass. The north-eastern scarp falls sharply away with the lower slopes covered in a belt of woodland. In places the surface is pitted as if struck by a thousand meteorites; these are shakeholes created by the slow dissolving of the underlying limestone. Man, too, has taken a hand in reshaping the landscape and evidence of quarrying will be seen as the walk progresses. Buzzards can be practically guaranteed to put in an appearance, red grouse feed off the heather, merlins hunt over the rough ground and I am told that peregrines regularly nest on the western side of the mountain. Smaller birds include wheatear and meadow pippit with sheep and hardy Welsh ponies grazing on the hillside.

Before setting out on the walk, take the track northwards through the car park for a short distance to visit the grave of Foxhunter, the champion international show jumper owned by Lt. Col. Sir Harry Llewellyn. Over two decades this great hearted horse was in the British show jumping team on no less than 35 occasions including the Gold Medal victory at the Helsinki Olympics in 1952. The horse carried his riders to victory in 78 international competitions and was as well known as any footballer or test cricketer of his day.

The Walk

From the top of the car park, take the path half right which picks its way through a tangle of tufted grass, heather, bilberry and small rocks with needle points of light reflected off their gritty surfaces. An easy ascent of 170 feet brings you to the summit plateau with its attendant triangulation point in just over three-quarters of a mile.

The view to the west includes Corn Du and Pen y Fan, the highest peaks of the Brecon Beacons, and the nearby spoil heaps of quarrying activities. To the north, a patterning of fields spreads out along the valley of the Usk, above which rises the shapely Sugar Loaf with the main path to the summit clearly etched upon its southern face. Table Mountain, with Crickhowell alongside the Usk, lies to the north-west, while the north-east offers the longest ridge of the Black Mountains and the topmost part of the holy mountain of Skirrid Fawr.

From the triangulation point, take the grassy path generally north-eastwards, heading in the direction of Skirrid Fawr (shown on the map as Ysgyryd Fawr) to bring you to the scarp edge in half a mile.

Here the westward scene is somewhat restricted but a bird's eye view of Abergavenny is added to the menu; Sugar Loaf remains and Skirrid Fawr is fully revealed. An addition to the entertainment may be provided by a close-up of the hang gliders who, apparently fearless, launch themselves off this cliff edge, some making the long glide down to the riverside.

From the scarp edge, swing right — heading southwards on a clear, winding, rutted track. In about a quarter of a mile, watch out for the lesser path which heads off diagonally left in a small hollow. As the hollow deepens, leave it to make a more comfortable descent by the well-defined path on

The Punchbowl, Blorenge

your left. The way heads towards a stone wall and continues downhill with it on your left, to reach a minor road just short of a cattle grid.

Do not go over the cattle grid but bear left on the wide track signed "Bridleway Llanfoist". Just beyond the gateway there is an information board describing the Punchbowl which is now in the care of the Woodland Trust. After passing the small plantation on your left, follow the broken stone wall on your right which edges a deepening hollow way overhung with gnarled old beech trees. As you will have learnt from the notice board these venerable beeches are a particularly attractive feature of this section of the walk. Keep the boundary wall/fence on your right with the path descending and eventually swinging sharp left and providing views to Abergavenny through the trees. The path is now soft underfoot, carpeted in generations of leaf mould.

The path emerges at the foot of the Punchbowl with a limpid pool first viewed through a veil of beech leaves. An eye set in the deep socket formed by glacial action, with a tiny island at the centre serving as its iris. Cross the bottom edge of the lake above which rises the steeply curving, tree-covered sides of the Punchbowl, an immensely attractive prospect.

Walkers who take this route in late May will be rewarded by the sight of successive carpets of bluebells to the south of the mountain wall with their heady scent drifting up the hillside.

From the end of the pool take the path that rises to a metal gateway and into a field. Head diagonally right over the field, noting the large "fairy ring" to your left. Continue with the boundary always to your right passing through several gateways and ignoring all paths waymarked downhill. There are excellent views to Abergavenny, the wooded hillsides and the Usk Valley. The path which has been heading generally northwards curves west and north-west as it passes above Cwm Craf where the scalloped slope rises to the scarp.

It was here that I once watched an aerial confrontation that went on for fully ten minutes. A buzzard upset by the presence of another bird of prey on its territory, a merlin I believe, was trying to chase it away. The smaller but much more agile merlin kept the buzzard at bay without difficulty until in the end the buzzard gave up.

What is clearly an old tramway is joined and the Sugar Loaf becomes more prominent dominating the view above the Usk Valley. The holes drilled into the rock to secure the rails are still evident and a tunnel or shaft is passed which nowadays offers bad weather shelter for sheep. The course of the old tramway eventually leads to the road, but our route leaves it three-quarters of a mile short of the Blaenavon Road so care is needed to spot the turn—especially in summer when the bracken is high.

Look for the conifer plantation that edges the tramway on the right. Shortly after this is met, take the narrow path that climbs half-left through the bracken. This is followed for just over half a mile. Two hundred yards after passing a spring, a junction is made with a broader track met by a small stone pillar. Turn right with the track and follow it south-westwards for a mile to reach the road after skirting the edge of Pen-fford-goch Pond. This is a man-made, but attractive stretch of water also known as Keepers Pond, which was built to provide a head of water to power the nearby ironworks.

From the pond follow the road southwards, towards Blaenavon and in 250 yards turn left to follow a narrow road which will return you to the Foxhunter car park in half a mile. **Note:** any attempt to cut across the moor from the pond back to the car park on seemingly promising paths is almost certain to lead you into very soggy ground.

ABERGAVENNY

WALK ONE – BLORENGE AND THE PUNCHBOWL

Abergavenny – Walk Two:
Blorenge – Summit Circuit

Starting Point: The Foxhunter car park on the southern flank of the mountain.

Access: From the A465 which passes south of Abergavenny, take the road signed to Llanfoist and Blaenavon, the B4246 and follow this for four miles. Turn left on the minor road to reach the car park opposite the wireless masts.

Distance: 3 miles.

Detail: An easy ascent to the summit which is continued to the north-eastern scarp with superb views.

Map: Outdoor Leisure Map 13.

This is a shortened version of Walk One which makes a pleasant evening stroll or a brief winter afternoon's escape to the hills. Only the route directions are given, for a fuller description please refer to the opening pages of the last walk.

The Walk

From the top of the car park take the path half right which gently rises for three-quarters of a mile to the triangulation point. Continue for a further half mile, heading generally north-easterly to reach the scarp edge with its views to Abergavenny, the Sugar Loaf, Skirrid Fawr and, more distantly, the Black Mountains. Turn right along the scarp edge joining the clear rutted track which descends south-westerly for three-quarters of a mile to reach a minor road. Here turn right and follow it for three-quarters of a mile to return to your starting point.

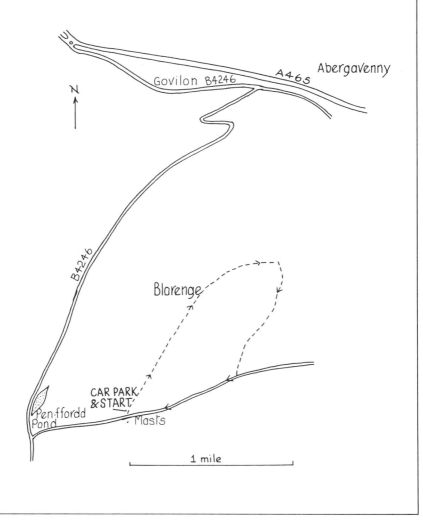

ABERGAVENNY

WALK TWO— BLORENGE·SUMMIT CIRCUIT

Abergavenny

Govilon B4246   A465

N

B4246

Blorenge

CAR PARK
& START

Pen·ffordd
Pond

Masts

1 mile

Abergavenny — Walk Three: The Sugar Loaf

Starting Point: Llwyn-du Roadside Rest.

Access: From the centre of Abergavenny, head westwards on the A40 signed Brecon, turn right on Chapel Road. Follow a narrowing lane to reach the car park just beyond High Beeches and a little short of Porth-y-Parc Farm.

Distance: 4½ miles.

Detail: A steady ascent through woods and bracken on clear paths, superb views from the summit with a long and enjoyable descent.

Map: Outdoor Leisure Map 13.

Toilets: Abergavenny otherwise none on route.

The Sugar Loaf is a little gem with a shapely profile that ensures instant recognition from afar. Walkers on the Malvern hills will point it out although it is 40 miles distant. Visitors to the Kymin Naval Temple above Monmouth will note it, a mere 16 miles away. It can also be seen from the Brecon Beacons. The mountain and much of the surrounding land is now in the care of the National Trust with paths leading to the summit from all points of the compass. This walk makes an approach from the south, follows the upper slopes on the east before climbing to the summit from the north.

The Walk

The small parking area at Llwyn-du provides a fine view to Abergavenny set beneath the hills, a taste of what is to come.

Two tracks run northwards from the car park, take the left-hand fork which rises between hedges soon to reach and pass a farm. Go straight ahead leaving the farm area by the left-hand gateway. Maintain your di-

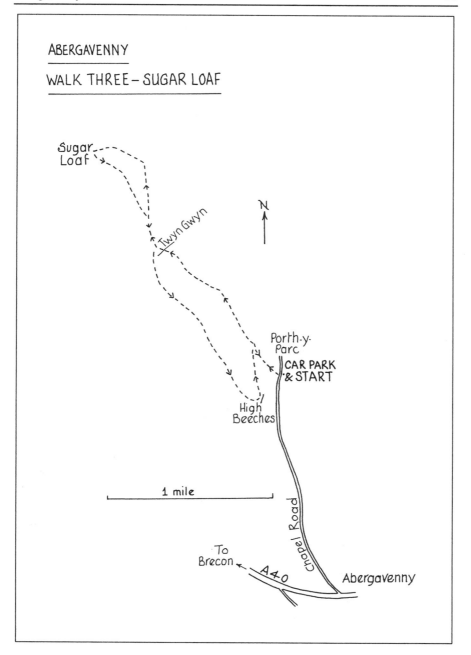

ABERGAVENNY

WALK THREE – SUGAR LOAF

Sugar Loaf

Twyn Gwyn

N

Porth-y-Parc

CAR PARK & START

High Beeches

1 mile

Chapel Road

To Brecon

A40

Abergavenny

rection with the wooded slopes of the Deri Ridge away to your right and the cone-topped Sugar Loaf seen ahead.

After a further gateway/stile the track soon divides but keep to the track which initially continues alongside a wire fence. The fence is left behind and the way passes through a further gateway and stile to bear diagonally left on a hollow way through a stretch of oak woodland — your direction is north-west. The track climbs steadily with gates and stiles at intervals. When the path again divides, continue with the left fork climbing to the south-west corner of the woodland; this lies just above the area marked on the map as The Park, with the remains of an old stone wall on your left.

At the edge of the wood, pass through three gateways/stiles in quick succession. On leaving the last stile go forward slight diagonally left with the Sugar Loaf seen chad-like over the next rise. The path climbs over an open grassy hill to cross the boundary of the National Trust property at Twyn Gwyn and on to the open hillside: rolling moorland with deep clefts

The Sugar Loaf from the south

cut by streams and covered in bracken, heather, bilberry and occasional stunted hawthorn.

The walk can be enjoyed at any time of the year but it is in autumn that the Sugar Loaf looks its best, with the middle slopes a waving sea of golden brown.

A number of paths come in from various directions. From the fence go forward for about 50 paces and then take the path heading slight diagonally right (north) which heads directly to the summit. Pursue this path for 300 yards only, then leave it to go forward to skirt the north-east side of the hill. The way narrows for a while but is seen clear and green through the bracken as it cuts across the flanks of the Sugar Loaf.

In just under half a mile, a wide track joins from the right. Continue your winding upward curve of the mountain heading towards its northern end and ignore the path which heads to the eastern side of the summit. When a clear track is met coming in over a spur from the northwest, you can turn left on this to make a steep and direct assault on the peak. Better still, continue on, swinging round the hill and rising steadily to the triangulation point with the National Trust logo.

If you have never once set foot within one of the Trust's stately homes, this hill top alone is sufficient justification for becoming a member.

This 1955 ft summit contrives to give the impression that every prospect pleases. Immediately below is a carpet of bracken broken by a network of paths. Woods climb the valley slopes wherever you turn, to the south the great bulk of Blorenge broods over Abergavenny, whose windows, catching the afternoon sun, sparkle like diamonds. In the northern arc the forests and moorland of the Black Mountains promise further good days on the hills. Four miles to the east the Holy Mountain of the Skirrid offers its own invitation and far away a clear day will point up the long line of the Malvern Hills. Not that they form the limit of our horizon for the view to the south extends to the Bristol Channel and beyond that silver thread to the heights of Exmoor.

To continue on your way head roughly south-easterly along the short summit from which Crickhowell and the River Usk can be seen. Now follow the path which, in half a mile, will return you to the boundary fence and gateway at Twyn Gwyn. On reaching the stile, two options are open to you: one is to return on your original approach but only if pressed for time or caught in bad weather.

A better route which gives a long descending view is recommended. Do not cross the stile but take the path with the fence line and the remains of a stone wall to your left, and follow this roughly south-eastwards. After nearly a mile, the boundary fence goes off at an angle but maintain your direction now descending more steeply. In about a quarter of a mile, the ruins of a building are seen beyond the fence which has now reappeared on your left. Continue for a few more yards then turn left along the fence line, first with a box hedge. An iron gateway is met, with no stile available the gate must be climbed. Go forward with the fence on your left and woodland to your right, with the path running just above a house shown on the map as High Beeches which was once the hunting lodge of the Marquess of Abergavenny. At the end of the wood, pass through a gateway by a large tree and follow an old track northwards (the farm, at Porth-y-parc will be seen to your right). Pass through a further metal gateway. Continue with the path falling gently through a wooded section to reach a north/south track, turn sharp right with this to return to your starting point in a quarter of a mile, by way of the farm passed on your outward journey.

Abergavenny – Walk Four: Ysgyryd Fawr

Starting Point: Layby to the south of the hill on the B4521 north-east of Abergavenny.

Distance: 3¼ miles

Detail: A climb through woodland and a moderately steep ascent with an excellent ridge walk.

Map: Outdoor Leisure Map 13.

Ysgyryd Fawr, the Skirrid, or the Holy Mountain as it is sometimes called, provides a short but rewarding outing. Occupying an isolated position above farmland it gives fine views from its comparatively modest height of 1595 ft and is not without an element of drama in its scenery. It derives its secondary name from an old legend which claims that the landslip, which is evident at the western end of the ridge, occurred at the time of the Crucifixion. This is a Welsh version of the rending of the veil of the temple in Jerusalem. Similar legends relating to split rocks and the like occur elsewhere. It is stretching the imagination beyond the bounds of reasonable elasticity to accept that the people of the area could have been aware of the events taking place on another green hill so far away. The Holy Mountain does, however, have a stronger religious connection. Scant remains of a church can be seen at the summit, where those of the catholic persuasion worshipped during periods of religious intolerance. Such was the respect for this place that at one time it was the custom to sprinkle soil gathered from the hill on coffins during the burial service. Beneath the hill, at Llanvihangel Crucorney, just off the A465, the oldest inn in Wales, The Skirrid, has a sign depicting the drama of the storm that raged over the mountain.

The Walk

From the layby take the broad track signed Skirrid Fawr which leads to Caer Wood. Once through the gate, take the stepped path ahead which, in spring, is lined with primroses, violets, wood anemone, celandine and wood sorrel. The path winds and climbs northwards for a quarter of a mile to reach a boundary wall and stile.

Once over the stile turn right and head along the flank of the hill. When the path divides after a short distance, ignore the left fork and continue on. The Skirrid rises steeply on your left but, to the south, there are wide views over a rolling green countryside with a scatter of farms and a long grey line of hills rising in a great arc in the distance.

Remain with the path beneath the hill for three-quarters of a mile, keeping the broken stone wall and fence on your right. As the ridge above your

Ysgyryd Fawr from The Skirrid Inn

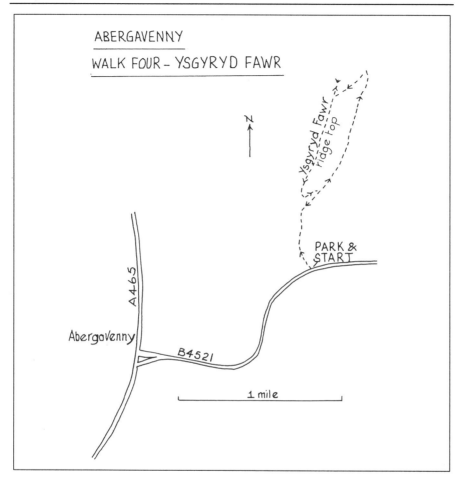

ABERGAVENNY

WALK FOUR - YSGYRYD FAWR

Ysgyryd Fawr
ridge top

N

PARK &
START

A465

Abergavenny

B4521

1 mile

head comes to an end, swing left up the hillside on a not very obvious path taking an oblique angle away from the north-eastern end of the summit — roughly south-west. When a T-junction of paths is met swing left on this climbing on a much clearer track which will take you to the summit ridge about 200 yards south of the triangulation point. Turn right along the ridge to the pillar where all that remains of the former St Michaels church will be noted.

This is a windy vantage point with a sheer drop on the northern side to ground made rough with a confusion of scattered rock.

Eyes raised to the hills offer the shapely Sugar Loaf and the long ridges of the Black Mountains.

From the 1595 ft summit, head south-westerly keeping to the crest of the falling ridge. This is the best part of the walk, the only regret being that it is not long enough so a leisurely progress is indicated for its full enjoyment. Abergavenny is seen in the valley with Blorenge rising steeply above the Usk.

After three-quarters of a mile, the deep cleft of the landslip is reached. The descent to the gap and a further rise can be negotiated to provide a viewpoint westwards and photographic opportunities for views back along the main ridge. Here again the Skirrid presents a wilder picture with the red sandstone laid bare on the steep slopes of the rift in the hill.

From the main ridge descend half left, (south), to meet the fence and turn right into the wood. When the stile in the wall is met, turn left and descend through the trees to your starting point.

A descent can also be made via the cleft in the landslip to reach the fenceline and turn right etc.,

The Black Mountains

Motorists driving towards Wales through the rolling Herefordshire countryside or heading down the Wye Valley will see to the west a great mountain wall – The Black Mountains. Black indeed they look from this angle whatever the season and black they can be in winter when the heather has faded and lies dead on the wet peaty moorland. Closer acquaintance will tell another story but first the walker needs to know a little of the geography of the area before setting out on what should prove to be a rewarding exploration.

Looking towards Table Mountain from the ancient Usk bridge at Crickhowell

Using the main roads as a guide, the Black Mountains lie within an area contained to the north-west by the A438 (and A4078) between Hay-on-Wye and Talgarth. The A479 running south from Talgarth to Crickhowell follows the western boundary with the Usk valley and the A40 as far as Abergavenny marking the southern boundaries. More loosely, the A465 between Hereford and Abergavenny, nears the hills as it crosses the border just beyond Pontrilas. Holding the line on the eastern side more tightly than the A465 is the unclassified road from Hay-on-Wye via Craswall and Longtown to Llanvihangel Crucorney. Within this box, minor roads and narrow lanes serve small villages and isolated farms. Many of these come to a dead end, others provide a loop such as the road which runs round the Olchon Valley or above Llanbedr. Have a care for this last one for there is an uncomfortably long narrow stretch, devoid of passing places. There is only one road that runs directly through the mountains – the 22-mile link between Hay-on-Wye and Abergavenny. This is a scenic route with, at its highest point, the Gospel Pass which descends to Capel-y-ffin, the Vale of Ewyas. Llanthony is a focal point for touring motorists and walkers alike.

The mountains are not as black as they are named. They rise steeply out of pleasant well-wooded valleys to a series of ridges – high, wild moorland grazed by both sheep and hardy Welsh ponies. They are variously and jointly clothed in grass, bracken, bilberry and heather together with, sometimes extensive, coniferous forest. As summer advances towards autumn, the hills gradually change colour. First, the grass of the upper slopes is bleached by the sun, then the splendour of the purpled heather and the reddening of the bilberry leaf. The valley trees cling briefly to their glad rags of yellow and bronze before wind and frost strip them bare and it is left to the golden-brown bracken to brighten winter days. Buzzards, ravens, and kestrels will be seen, perhaps the occasional grouse, day hunting owls heard and the aerial activity increased by mans conquest of engineless flight – gliders, hang-gliders and parascenders along the northern scarp.

The ridges vary in the views they offer; the wider plateaus may exclude the valley but compensate with fine skyscapes or mountain

On Black Hill, looking over the Olchon Valley to The Black Mountains

profiles and then relent with cameo glimpses of the farms below. The ridge ends and scarp edges, especially to the north offer wide ranging prospects in generous measure. There are generally good clear, but sometimes soggy, paths over the summits with some routes signed and waymarked out of the valleys. There are more paths on the ground than appear on the maps; some which look promising prove to be no more than disappearing sheep walks, others which at first are less distinct may make important links. A working knowledge of the layout of the valleys and the mountains that divide them is soon gained, but a general description may be useful to newcomers.

The ridges push out from a seven-mile escarpment running north-easterly above the Wye Valley from Pengenffordd but are listed here from east to west. Starting in Herefordshire, there is the short but delightful Black Hill ridge above the Olchon Valley. From

Hay Bluff the longest, usually called the Hatterrall Ridge, runs for more than twelve miles before the road is found again at Pandy; it carries the Offa's Dyke Path along the English/Welsh border, peaking at 2306 ft. The Gospel Pass now intervenes, to the west of which rises Lord Herefords Knob, or more succinctly, Twmpa 2264 ft. From here a three-mile spur runs down to Capel-y-ffin and the eight-mile long Vale of Ewyas with Llanthony Priory set mid-way – a useful launching-off point for the walker.

To the west of Llanthony rises Bal Mawr, a ridge upon a ridge, which has its beginnings on Pen Rhos Dirion and continues above the Grwyne Fawr valley and over Garn Wen. The next ridge is much more complicated – it has its beginnings at the top of Cwm Cwmstab and rises to Waun Fach, at 2660 ft the highest point of the Black Mountains. It continues over Pen y Gadair Fawr, Pen Twyn Mawr and on to Crug Mawr. The ridge splits at Waun Fach with a spur running out to Pen Trumau, then south over Mynydd Llysiau and Pen Twyn Glas below which lies the remote upper Grwyne Fechan valley. A further link from Pen Twyn Glas runs south over the dramatic heights of Pen Allt-mawr (2359 ft). From here, a descent is made to the hill fort on Table Mountain (1479ft) which in turn looks down upon Crickhowell and the valley of the Usk.

The northern scarp can be explored in a continuous passage over the tops of Hay Bluff to Pengenffordd via Twmpa, Pen Rhos Dirion, Y Das, Y Grib and finally the hill fort on Castell Dinas. Paths running under the peaks can be used to complete both long and short circuits.

Good roads put the Black Mountains in reach for day walkers from a wide area. Weekenders, or longer holiday makers will find Abergavenny, Crickhowell and Hay-on-Wye useful bases; bed and breakfast accommodation will also be found in the smaller villages.

The Black Mountains – Walk One: Black Hill and Offa's Dyke Path

Starting Point: Black Hill picnic site.

Access: Leave the A465 (Hereford/Abergavenny road) at Pontrilas taking the B4347 signed to Ewyas Harold where it is left to follow several miles of narrow lanes via Longtown and Llanveynoe into the Olchon Valley to the south-east end of Black Hill. The picnic site is signed to the right about half a mile after passing Tir Bill Farm.

Distance: 8½ miles.

Detail: A steep ascent to a fine ridge walk thence on to join Offa's Dyke Path to return over a moorland plateau with a descent to the Olchon Valley.

Map: 1:25,000 Outdoor Leisure Map No. 13.

The Black Mountains are not exclusively in Wales: the border lies along the centre of the broad ridge from Hay Bluff towards Hatterrall Hill, with the mountains spilling over into a remote and beautiful corner of Herefordshire.

Whatever magic may be conjured up in the mind by the inclusion of a section of the Offa's Dyke Path, it is Black Hill which makes the outing a little gem. So much so that an excursion to the triangulation point will provide a scenic and rewarding round trip of about three miles. For a description of a circular route please see Walk Two.

The Walk

From the car park cross the stile and strike up the hillside with its scatter of gorse bushes. The steepening slope is marked by the tread of boots, which now provide a stepped path to ease the way. The wide views which have been apparent from the picnic site rapidly improve. A small grassy plateau serves as an observation point before a further ascent leads on to an outcrop of rock from which suitably dramatic photographs may be

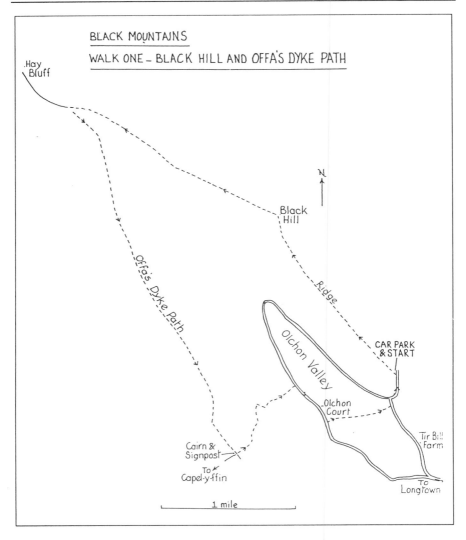

BLACK MOUNTAINS

WALK ONE - BLACK HILL AND OFFA'S DYKE PATH

composed. The hill now narrows to a sharp edge, rocky underfoot and dropping quickly away on either side.

To the west are the impressive cliff-like slopes of the Hatterrall Ridge over which the Offa's Dyke Path makes a long passage, closely following the boundary between England and Wales. Beneath the protection of this great green wall is the Olchon Valley, through which a narrow lane serves the isolated farms. From your viewpoint a clearly defined zig-zag path falling off the hillside will be noted, this is part of the return route. The Olchon Brook fed by a series of springs issuing out of the steep slopes tumbles down the well-wooded valley. The trees do not persist for long, giving up the uneven struggle for a foothold as the land rises until only an occasional gallant hawthorn stubbornly remains. The brook has but a short course to run for it loses its identity as it joins the Monnow at Longtown.

To your right, and far below, lies the Monnow Valley, seemingly more orderly than the sheep country of the Olchon. The Monnow, reinforced by the Olchon Brook, forms the boundary between England and Wales until it achieves full Welsh nationality, lending its name to the historic town of Monmouth where it joins the Wye.

Scramble up the rocky pavement and follow the narrow ridge north-west for a mile and a quarter to the triangulation point.

Indeed there is nowhere else to go, for only the sure-footed sheep can do otherwise. Even they are sufficiently impressed for one of their number to be occasionally observed standing upon a rocky outcrop playing `King of the Castle'.

The shiny structures which catch the sun to your right form part of the Satellite Earth Station, ten miles distant at Kingstone. Part way along the ridge, a cairn is passed with a small bad weather shelter.

As height is gained a further ridge is seen to the left and with it the distinctive table, or stepped shape, of Pen y Gadair Fawr (2625 ft). To the north of it lies Waun Fach, less shapely from this angle, but by virtue of its extra 33 feet, this is the highest point in the Black Mountains.

The ridge widens as it approaches the triangulation point (2100 ft) with the now grassy path advancing through heather and bilberry.

In the eastern arc, the nine-mile long range of the Malvern Hills may be identified, 30 miles distant. To the north beyond Kington rises the Hergest Ridge, the rounded slopes of Bradnor Hill, said to have the highest golf course in Europe, and the Radnor Forest.

From the triangulation point head roughly north-west passing shallow pools of water on a narrow but clear path which widens as progress is made. Sharp pointed rushes rise above the peaty water like Mohican style haircuts. The scenery as you advance in the direction of Hay Bluff invites comparison with the North York Moors. Tiny matchstick figures may be seen on the skyline as they trek up the ridge.

There is a division of paths at a Y-junction but they join together after only a short distance. The north-westerly direction is maintained without interruption for a mile and a half. The path then makes a slight curve to the left; this should be watched for as you draw roughly level with the distinctive New House Wood. As you advance the top edge of a forest will be seen on the western hillside ahead and the end of the ridge which terminates in Twmpa, more colourfully known as Lord Hereford's Knob.

If it is a weekend it is almost certain that for some time now you will have been observing the activities in the sky of a flock of colourful 'birds' not designed by nature – hang gliders, parachutists and other aerial adventurers.

The curving path connects with a track running at an angle across a shallow depression. To the right it leads to Hay Bluff but our way is to the left, with an immediate climb to higher ground. In fine weather the way from the top of the mound, roughly southwards, is clear – navigation in mist is quite another matter.

Offa's Dyke Path is joined and followed for the next two and a half miles over a grassy plateau with, as befits its moorland character, some soggy areas to dodge round.

There are great contrasts in the landscape to be seen, from the wild tops of the upper profiles of the Black Mountain ridges, the rough moorland gives way to the gently rolling farming country of Herefordshire. The nearest ridge to the right is that running from Lord Hereford's Knob which tends to be lost against the background as it descends to Capel-y-ffin.

Soon the Black Hill ridge is seen to the left, and ahead the Holy Mountain – Ysgyryd Fawr – comes into view beyond Hatterrall Hill.

At intervals, cairns with signless posts blown down by the wind will be noted, relics of past efforts to assist the walker on his way. The difficulty of following this long ridge end to end in bad weather will be quickly apparent: in cloud, there are no landmarks and, once off the path, finding it again will need both luck and judgment. One possible problem has been resolved with the provision of a series of closely linked cairns over a section of the way where the erosion has widened out to create a mini desert.

The paths which lead off the plateau are indistinct and easily missed, but a cairn and signpost mark our path left to the Olchon Valley and right for Capel-y-ffin. Given the fate of the other posts along the way, the need to watch for more permanent landmarks is obvious.

The narrow and indistinct path bears left off the ridge but improves as the descent steepens. Before long, you will probably be able to see the windscreen of your car sparkling in the sun. The path now takes a zig-zag course down the almost cliff-like slopes. Black Hill is seen to perfection with the long airy prospect of the Olchon Valley likely to be remembered with pleasure for some time to come.

Heading up the ridge of Black Hill

The rocky path continues between bracken to a crossroad of paths, the left and forward of which are indistinct. Turn sharp right on the wider path and turn left with this in a little over 100 yards. When the fence line is met keep this on your left as you continue downhill.

Pass through a gateway at the bottom of the field to a lane after crossing a further short field. Turn right along the lane with the hedge hung with honeysuckle.

Olchon Court with its barns walled and tiled in stone is passed in 300 yards and the name ingeniously posted upon the wall in recycled materials. A discarded metal gate forming the base on which the legend is picked out in horseshoes. Beyond, old millstones form a part of the enclosure wall.

The lane now falls steeply to reach Beilibach in a further 300 yards. Turn left through the gateway passing the farmhouse to your right and continue over a stile. Go forward over the field to descend to the Olchon Brook which is crossed by a footbridge hidden beneath the trees.

Once over the brook climb the grassy bank and follow the field edge with trees on your right. Towards the top of the field, the narrow path ducks under the trees and soon crosses a trickle of a stream, thence left up the hillside passing the barn of Black Hill Farm on your right. Take the track which curves to the right to join a metalled way which rises to a lane. Here turn left and at the next junction turn right to return to your starting point.

Literary note: readers may recall a television adaptation some years ago of Bruce Chatwin's novel "On the Black Hill". Now that the location has been visited the book may be read with special pleasure. It tells the irreversibly intertwined life story of twin boys who lived in this border country with close attention to detail which adds greatly to its charm.

The Black Mountains – Walk Two: Black Hill

Starting Point: Black Hill Picnic Site.

Access: Leave the A465 (Hereford/Abergavenny road) at Pontrilas taking the B4347 as far as Ewyas Harold. Some miles of narrow lanes are then followed via Longtown and Llanveynoe into the Olchon Valley thence to the south-east end of Black Hill. The picnic site is signposted to the right about half a mile after passing Tir Bill Farm.

Distance: 4½ miles

Detail: The lower slopes of Black Hill are followed until a steep ascent leads on to the shoulder linking with the main body of the Black Mountains, thence a long and rewarding descent along the Black Hill spine.

Map: 1:25,000 Outdoor Leisure Map No. 13.

This route is a shorter version of Walk One with the added pleasure of the long passage over the descending ridge. If you are based at Hay-on-Wye it is possible to reach the starting point of this excursion via the lane that leads to Craswall. Those passing through Longtown may care to pause for a few minutes to visit its twelfth century castle – no charge for admission. The remains of its outer walls give access to the mound on which stands its circular keep. From this elevated position there are excellent views of the Olchon Valley and the long eastern ridge of the Black Mountains. This timeless landscape receives a sudden and noisy lurch into this century when a low flying jet fighter zips up the valley and over the mountain tops.

The Walk

The view from the car park is superb: below lies the valley with fields climbing the slopes until they abandon the uneven battle and

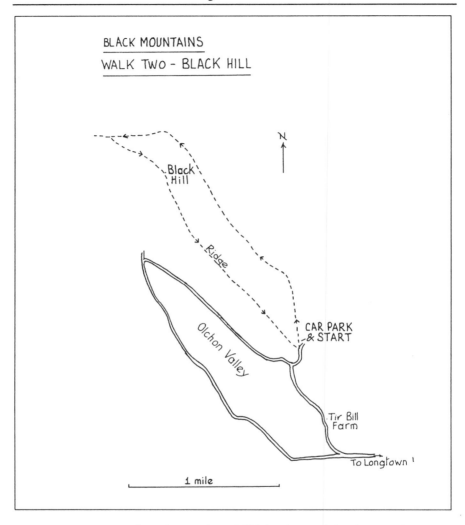

BLACK MOUNTAINS

WALK TWO - BLACK HILL

Black Hill

Ridge

N

Olchon Valley

CAR PARK & START

Tir Bill Farm

To Longtown

1 mile

grass gives way to bracken. The cliff-like face of the long ridge is so steep that paths coming off the hills take, of necessity, a zig-zag course to ease the descent. Black Hill starts on a wide base but soon narrows to a tent-like structure. It is tempting to search for descriptive phrases like `knife edge' – almost true – for at its narrowest point it is only a foot or two wide – say a blunt knife's edge. A small adventure that is deferred for the return leg.

From the Black Hill picnic site go forward to the stile but instead of turning up the hill, take the bridleway which follows its eastern flanks.

It is an old road, lined with gnarled hawthorn, rutted by the passage of tractors which have surely widened the narrower wheel tracks made by farm carts of earlier generations. Four hundred and fifty feet above your head the knobbly spine of Black Hill is sharply outlined whilst to your right the views are of a wider farming landscape.

The track heads for Craswall and beyond, but we leave it about 700 yards from the car park. Small trickles of water are crossed almost unnoticed but, after a more definite stream is forded, take the indistinct path through bracken which is found on the left in about 100 yards.

The path climbs steadily at an angle to the hill, dipping in and out of a series of small gullies. The general direction is north-west and the initial objective is to contour the hillside, well under the ridge, passing round and under the summit at its northern end. (Ignore the path which will be seen striking up to the centre of the ridge).

The path levels out after a while and pursues a generally level course through bracken and open patches of grass, with the direction of travel indicated by the path seen well ahead at intervals.

As you draw level with the end of Black Hill the way curves round it, climbs a little before levelling out again with a clear path seen on the higher slopes forward left.

Just after crossing a distinct watercourse a path will be met coming up the hillside, take it rising diagonally left which broadens and steepens considerably.

Close to the top, a rock makes a fine viewpoint and a suitable spot for one of those fearless "mountain goat" photographs featured in the outdoor magazines but with little risk to life and limb. In such pictures, the photographer scrambling to position himself for the best effect is often at greater hazard than his subject!

When the rim of the plateau is reached, carry on along the side of a gully still gaining height. At the top of the gully, go forward for a few yards to a crossing path, then turn left to follow it for just under half a mile to the triangulation point on the 2100 ft north-western summit of Black Hill.

On Black Hill, overlooking the Monnow Valley

The views are wide ranging. Spread out below is the huge "ridge and furrow" effect as you look across the grain of the landscape of the lower hills of Herefordshire and Gwent. A fine rolling countryside broken by the pattern of field enclosures that changed the landscape as the agrarian revolution advanced. The greater mechanization of farming following the war reversed the clock in many parts of the country as prairie-type fields were needed to achieve maximum efficiency. Not so in this border area where the chequer board laid out in previous centuries continues to delight the eye from above. The distant view always prompts the most speculation – to the east the Malvern Hills, the northern arc includes Shropshire's Clee Hills and the Radnor Forest area of Powys. Nearer at hand a succession of wooded hills conceals the course of the Wye as it winds between Hay and Hereford. The Black Mountains view is more restricted. The long green ridge above the Olchon Valley topped by the shadowy grey profile beyond the table-topped Pen y Gadair Fawr – the only easily recognisable landmark.

Now starts the superb return on what is one of the best of the Black Mountain ridges. Unlike some of the ridges where the plateau is wider and the views sometimes more confined, Black Hill has no such constraints.

From the triangulation point take the path over the narrowing summit to join the ridge. A long slow passage is made over a series of widely spaced steps – rocky risers and grassy treads heading south-easterly with the slopes shelving steeply away on either side.

The Olchon Valley is seen to perfection and beyond Hatterrall Hill at the end of the companion ridge the hills range away into the grey haze. Below to your left, the paths that looked so indistinct on the ground weave a thread of lighter green between the acres of bracken and on a good day you may even be able to spot the distant smudge that marks the Cotswolds. Now is the time to put away the book and enjoy the rest of the walk to the full, with the ridge running on to a final stone pavement from which a steep descent is made to the car park.

The Black Mountains – Walk Three:
Lord Hereford's Knob

Starting Point: Small car park on the Gospel Pass on the eastern slope of Lord Hereford's Knob.

Access: Via the minor road running south from Hay-on-Wye or via the Vale of Ewyas.

Distance: 7 miles approx.

Detail: Ridge walk over grass and heather moorland with a very steep ascent at the start of the return leg.

Map: 1:25,000 Outdoor Leisure Map No. 13

Hay-on-Wye, now justly famous as a leading centre of the second-hand book market, is also the welcoming northern gateway to the Black Mountains. It is a convenient departure point for this walk.

Leave the town by the single track road signed to Abergavenny and follow this for about five and a half miles to find the small car park on the Gospel Pass. It is a true mountain road, narrow and winding, with sheep and hill ponies grazing on the unfenced common land. A road that quickens the pulse, instilling an anticipatory sense of adventure in the walker as the mountains are approached. In winter, water leaching out of the hillsides quickly freezes to make a decorative lace edging that spells danger for the incautious driver.

Ignore the first car park by the stone circle (note there is often a tea van here) and continue for a mile and a quarter. The twin guardians of the pass, Hay Bluff and Twmpa, otherwise known as Lord Hereford's Knob, rise sharply to over 2200 ft.

Gospel Pass is a translation from the Welsh, Bwlch-yr-Efengel, and it is easy to assume that this has reference to the Priory at Llanthony, an Augustinian foundation dating from the early years of the twelfth century. An old legend has it that Saint Peter and Saint Paul travelled this way spreading the gospel of Christ. A nice concept but unfortunately, exemplary correspondent that Paul was, there is no epistle to the Welsh to be found in the New Testament. Llanthony Priory is featured in another walk, but the turning point of this route gives a distant view of the remains of the monastery – Llanthony Abbey – established in 1870 by the Reverend Joseph Leycester Lyne – of whom more elsewhere. The addition of the two small chapels at Capel-y-ffin does nothing to ease the confusion of the origins of the naming of the Gospel Pass. Not that the list should stop here for there may well be a connection with the great evangelistic tour of Wales made in 1188 by the Archbishop of Canterbury to rally support for the crusade to the Holy Land.

The Walk

The path starts about 150 paces north of the car park, but the access is a muddy turmoil and further use will not improve it. To avoid it, take the grassy path on the right (as you face away from Hay-on-Wye) which winds up the hill soon to join the track which runs close to the scarp edge. The top is reached after three-quarters of a mile and 500 feet of ascent, with a fine reward for moderate effort.

There is no triangulation point to mark Twmpa's 2263 ft summit, that is an honour accorded to its companions, Hay Bluff and Pen Rhos Dirion, but a series of cairns assists navigators in poor weather. There are fine views down to the commons and pastures where ant-like sheep graze amongst the grass and bracken and people reputedly seek out the so-called magic mushrooms. More distantly the River Wye may be glimpsed, and perhaps fleetingly an RAF jet zipping upstream, today's high technology dragon fly. Across the Gospel Pass is the fine prospect of Hay Bluff with its northern face and table-topped ridge over which the Offa's Dyke Path makes a long passage.

When this route was walked in mid-February, the valley gardens were showing promise of an early spring with snowdrops and crocus in bloom and daffodils beginning to show their heads. Not so on the mountains, here winter still held the world in its grip of

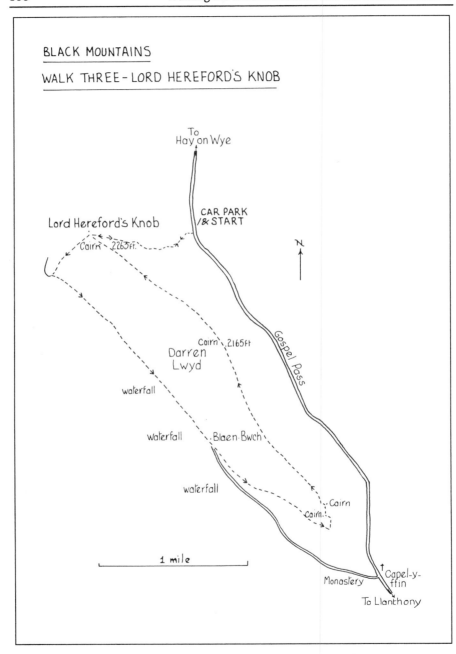

BLACK MOUNTAINS

WALK THREE - LORD HEREFORD'S KNOB

To Hay on Wye

CAR PARK /& START

Lord Hereford's Knob

Cairn ~ 2263 ft.

N

Cairn 2165ft

Darren Lwyd

Gospel Pass

waterfall

waterfall   Blaen Bwch

waterfall

Cairn

Cairn

1 mile

Monastery   Capel-y-ffin

To Llanthony

iron. Water draining through the turf had frozen into crystal sta-
lactites and our boots shattered a thousand tiny icy mirrors on the
uneven ground. Walkers following the Offa's Dyke path from
Pandy to Hay at this time of the year pass through three or even
four climates in the couple of hours it takes to reach the town
from the top of the bluff.

From the summit, head roughly south-west for 700 yards, losing about
200 feet of height, to a grassy bridleway. Here turn left and follow it for one
and a half miles to the farm at Blaen Bwch. A fine path runs in the fold between two long ridges. Soon a stream is joined; keep this to your right as it
falls down the hillside with an occasional waterfall to speed it on its way.

After a while the stream drops into a deep cleft which it has dug for itself
by centuries of hard work. Our path rises above it, although on occasion it
runs as wetly but fortunately not as deeply as the stream.

As Blaen Bwch is reached several gates have to be negotiated, and a notice requests walkers' cooperation in keeping strictly to the paths in this
area. Beyond the farm keep to the track for about 300 yards. As the fence
on the right comes down to the road, veer left a little and go forward on a
path for a further three-quarters of a mile. The path rises steadily with
good views ahead and of the valley below through which the stream has
departed soon to add its contribution to the Afon Honddu at Capel-y-ffin.

The path runs along the flank of the hill, above the valley with the occasional distant bark of a dog or cock crow carried up from the farms below.

After crossing a small streamlet (not shown on the map and probably dry
at times) the path divides. Ignore the right fork which runs downhill and
continue. As you round the end of the hill with a full view down the valley
towards Llanthony, look for the grassy path on the left which climbs
steeply. Again watch for the sharp bend to the left which leads to a rock
outcrop making a natural seat. From here bear right to climb to a cairn
about 150 yards ahead. From this point a second cairn will be seen which
is reached by a narrow but clear path. There is a handsome prospect of
the valley with the dark walls of the incomplete chapel in stark contrast
with the white painted monastery buildings. Above the Gospel Pass a
patch of forest climbs the hillside, its boundaries shaped like a pullover
hung out to dry.

The walk now returns to the summit of Twmpa over the wide ridge of
Darren Lwyd. The path which runs between tufted grass and heather is

not always distinct but in clear weather presents no real problems during the two and a half miles. Occasional wet patches will be encountered but these will not cause booted walkers any concern. A small cairn is sited at roughly the half-way point. Beyond this, there is a stretch of eroded moorland where small rocks dot the bare surface which shades from silver grey to black peat before the path is again seen running ahead.

After enjoying the view from the summit, make your way downhill to the car park by your outward route.

The southern end of Darren Llwyd ridge from Capel-y-ffin

The Black Mountains – Walk Four: Hatterrall Hill, Offa's Dyke Path and the Crooked Church

Starting Point: Queens Head Inn.

Access: Leave the A465 at Llanvihangel Crucorney following the Llanthony road for 1½ miles. A walkers' car park is on the left just beyond the Inn – a small charge is made.

Distance: 8 miles.

Detail: Steady climb to Upper Pentwyn then Offa's Dyke Path ridge walk with return by bridleway and field paths via Cwmyoy church.

Map: 1:25,000 Outdoor Leisure Map No. 13.

This walk can be enjoyed at any time of the year but it makes a good winter excursion with the passage along the ridge accomplished in the first half of the day. The Offa's Dyke Path track is clear enough but the lack of good landmarks on the ridge requires careful attention to the map especially in hazy weather to identify routes off the hill.

Snow lies in patches on the upper slopes long after it has departed from the valley bottoms and, when lit by the low sun, makes a brilliant contrast of white carpets laid over a golden-brown floor of bracken. Temperatures which may be comfortable in the valleys are appreciably lower on the tops, even without the wind chill factor, and the frost may maintain an iron grip on the landscape throughout the day. Ice crackles under foot and the blackened heather is hung with rime. Extra clothing is essential and the balaclava should not be despised for even moderate winds quickly chill the cheeks. After following this route one fine January day we paused for refreshment by Cwmyoy church and, taking the plastic drinks bottle from the

rucksack, found it partly iced. Nevertheless, pick the right day and
you will be well rewarded.

The Walk

From the Queens Head, take the lane signed `Cwmyoy 1 mile' which de-
scends to cross the Afon Honddu by a little two-arched bridge. Continue
with the lane ignoring the signed path to Crucorney to a T-junction in
about 200 yards. Bear left but take the path immediately on the right,
passing a stone barn.

With the stream on your left make your way up the hillside, soon passing
through a patch of woodland. At the top of the first field beyond the
wooded area, cross a stile and go forward and in 200 yards over a further
stile taking the path rising through light woodland. Exit by a metal gateway and continue to the farm buildings of Upper Pentwyn seen ahead.
Here the retrospective views have widened to include the green pastures
rising up the opposite hillside, broken by hedgerows and small clumps of
woodland, giving way to upper slopes clothed in bracken.

Pass the farm buildings on your right to a broad track, swing right with this
to pass the empty farm house and barn. Head eastwards to the gate seen
ahead (200 yards). Beyond the gate a clear track is met, cross this to join,
in 15 paces, the grassy rutted track which is the Offa's Dyke Path. Turn
left, heading north. (Looking back down the path the earth walls of an old
hill fort will be noted).

Edged by bracken at first which soon gives way to a wide carpet of
heather, the rising track passes a large stone walled enclosure to your
left. The eastern valley is now in sight, far below flows the river Monnow
and the tiny settlement of Oldcastle (ahead). Just the church, a few buildings, a couple of yew trees and a Cedar of Lebanon.

The triangulation point (1552 ft) is reached in just under three-quarters of
a mile after joining the ridge with further views to Oldcastle. Continue
northwards with the sometimes curving Offa's Dyke Path for two miles.
The path to Oldcastle (not our route) is signposted in about a quarter of a
mile and cairns mark other, sometimes indistinct, paths.

Hardy red grouse zoom swift and low over the heather, not de-
serting the tops even in the hardest weather. They feed almost exclusively off the plant and must live where their larder is.

BLACK MOUNTAINS

WALK FOUR – HATTERRALL HILL VIA OFFA'S DYKE PATH & THE CROOKED CHURCH

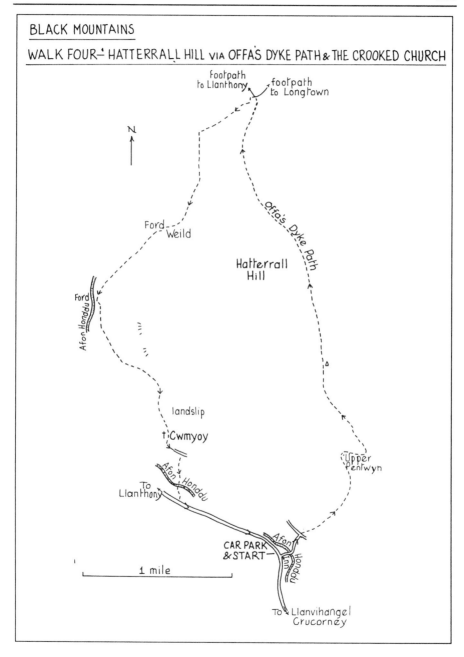

The point at which the Offa's Dyke Path is abandoned is close to the old path which rises from Llanthony and descends to Longtown but is not currently signposted — Grid ref: 308270. The required and not very visible path on the left is marked by a small cairn just short of the Longtown crossing. Wayfinding is a little easier if you take the diagonal path — north-west — that has climbed from Llanthony. Follow this for only 70 paces, then swing left on a narrower way which in a short distance meets a stone wall.

Turn left with the wall which very shortly makes a right angle, continue with the line of the wall descending for about 200 yards. By now the path has become clear, leaving the wall and falling south of west. There are views up the valley to Llanthony Priory with the descent being made in the general direction of the large farm at Maes-y-Beran. (Note the edge of an almost buried stone wall enclosure is passed immediately right, shortly followed by a narrow track which crosses your path — both help to confirm you are on the right way).

The path descends to reach a metal gate (about 600 yards after leaving the ridge) and continues between fences to reach a roughly north-south bridleway at the fence line. Turn left to follow the bridleway southwards for three-quarters of a mile to the now deserted settlement of Weild — initially with the fence to your right, later on your left.

Cross the ford at Weild and, after passing through the scatter of farm buildings, proceed on the waymarked path south-westerly through the fields for a little over half a mile to reach the footbridge over the Honddu. **Do not cross the bridge;** Instead, go forward over a stile, faintly waymarked "To the Hill", and follow the broad track which rises through woodland. Here, and further on, there are glimpses of the sheer, wild sandstone cliffs of Darren to your left.

The track curves left along the fence line to a stile on the right. From here go forward over a field to the farm at Daren Uchaf, passing through a gateway and following the track between the farmhouse and the outbuildings. Continue curving left up a slope on a good track to pass a later farmhouse on your right. Go through gateway/stile and when a crossing path is met continue on the broad rising track curving slightly left. At the top of a short rise there are further views of the rocky cliffs of Darren.

Swing right on the track which in 200 yards passes through a gateway and over a stream with buildings to your right. Beyond the stream take the path ahead, which in winter at least, does duty for a stream for a short distance. Keep the fence line on your right, after a short distance the path divides at a metal gateway. Ignore the half left track which passes to the east of the volcano-like hill seen ahead and continue along the fence line. Pass through a wooden gateway descending with fences either side and soon passing a corrugated iron and wooden building. When the path again divides, take the right falling path and after passing through a further gateway continue between stone walls to Cwmyoy Church.

The church was built beneath the site of a dramatic landslip when the hill behind it was cleft in two. Its survival is quite remarkable; tilted at a crazy angle, it is now firmly buttressed against further misfortune. Within, the church is welcoming with the light bouncing off the cream washed walls and a simple wooden altar. There are many slate memorials, one a sad inscription for "Joan, daughter of Mr. Williams of Sharpal, she died 19th July 1781, aged 3 years".

In the chancel there is an even earlier memorial, the rhyming lines of the inscription overflow for lack of space mingling in confused fashion until a careful reading restores the metre:

"Thomas Price he takes his nap
In our common mother's lap
Waiting to hear the bridegroom say
Away my dear, come away
1682"

Around the church clusters a little group of whitewashed houses, a pleasing picture of this small community which has tenaciously occupied this remote hillside for so long.

From the church descend to the road by the kissing gate and path. Turn left passing what for the moment at least is one of the few remaining red telephone boxes – specially retained in conservation areas. Just beyond the box bear right and follow the lane downhill. As the road levels out, take the path on the right, signed "Queens Head 1km", which falls gently to reach the river. Once over the footbridge, bear half left, then right up the slope. From there, go over a stile and a short field to the road by a square bungalow.

A backward glance shows Cwmyoy in its setting on the slopes beneath the landslip. Turn left down the road to return to your starting point at the Queens Head. In winter, the road offers views to the river which are largely obscured during the summer.

The Black Mountains:
Llanthony – Shades of the Past

The little winding road that carries the traveller from Hay-on-Wye into the Black Mountains at last descends into the Vale of Ewyas. The road narrows even more as the hedges close in and the motorist must have a care for oncoming traffic and a memory for the last passing place. Whatever views there may be to the hills are not for him and Llanthony may be reached with a small feeling of relief. Beneath the bolder type the map makers have added in brackets Llanddewi Nant Hodni – the church of St. David by the Honddu stream and this is where our story begins.

David, destined to become the patron saint of Wales, is reputed to have been the son of a Welsh chieftain. He preached the cause of Christianity during the sixth century, establishing a number of monasteries across the southern part of the country and is credited with the establishment of a chapel or hermitage at Llanthony. The calendar moves on five hundred and fifty years to the early days of the twelfth century. The Normans, following their invasion of 1066, found the border country, like the Romans before them, troubled territory. With schizophrenic devotion, they built great castles to tighten their grip on this world and endowed monasteries in the hope of securing a foothold in the next.

The de Lacy family had been established in the valley from the early days of the Conquest. The story goes that in 1100 one of their number, William, was hunting in the well-wooded valley when he took cover from a storm in the remains of David's chapel. While there, like Paul on the road to Damascus, he experienced a sudden religious conversion which led to a dramatic change in his lifestyle. He gave up his place at the court, abandoned wealth and privileges and settled at Llanthony to pursue a life of quiet contemplation.

In a year or two, he was joined by the Queen's chaplain, Ernisus. A church was built and a small community of like-minded men formed the early band of Augustinians. Eighty years after William's conversion, work began on the large priory, now roofless but with eight handsome arches still intact to serve as a reminder of the quality of workmanship that went into its construction.

It was in the lenten days of the year 1188 that Archbishop Baldwin made his arduous and successful tour of Wales, gathering support for the third Crusade to the Holy Land, in the course of which he called at Llanthony. With him was Giraldus – Gerald of Wales, Archdeacon of Brecon – who set down the story of the difficult mission in *Itinerarium Cambrense*. Despite the heavy demands of the journey he found time, magpie like, to assemble some of the folklore of the countryside through which he passed – stories which continue to appear in today's guides. He devoted a fair amount of space to Llanthony, referring to its origins, development and endowment. He described the construction, enthused upon the healthy environment and commended its suitability for those disposed to the contemplative life; he was critical of the daughter house at Gloucester, which he felt was more concerned with the things of this world. His dissertation upon the pursuit of worldly goods would not sound amiss if delivered from today's pulpit.

The Archbishop and Gerald went on their way, making the sign of the cross over the volunteers who flocked to the cause. 1189 saw the accession to the throne of Richard I; Baldwin was there to place the crown upon his head. In March of the following year, practising what he had preached Baldwin left on the crusade for which he had so assiduously campaigned. He did not return.

The life and work of the Priory continued through good times and bad for a further three hundred and fifty years, until the dissolution in 1538 when the few remaining members of the community were pensioned off and the buildings passed into the hands of Henry VIII's commissioners. The following centuries of neglect took their inevitable toll.

That might well have been the end of the story, but as we have seen this remote valley has an uncanny capacity for attracting mystics and those of a romantic turn of mind. In 1809, the author Walter Savage Landor puchased the Priory. Forestry, sheep breeding and a new school were amongst his plans. Two years later, it was a case of love at first sight when he met the daughter of a Swiss banker. Unhappily neither the farming enterprise or the marriage prospered and financial pressures forced the sale of the estate and Landor to spend most of the rest of his life in Italy.

The Abbot's House, Llanthony Priory

The eloquent ruins of the Priory with the view to the hills through its great curving arches should not divert the visitor from the parish church of St. David. Within, it is quietly impressive, larger than might be imagined from its outward appearance. Unspoken history hangs silently on the chill air. Above the pulpit a stained glass memorial window to Charles Knight, DFC depicts St. David in the setting of Llanthony with the church and priory. Slate tablets commemorate the people of the vale, Price, Williams, Jones, Lewis, Parry and Davis. Beneath the memorial to John and Mary Trumper is set the brief exhortation – "My debts are paid, my grave you see, Therefore prepare to follow me".

A gloomy thought on which to leave but, as Benjamin Franklin asserted, there are only two things certain in this life – death and taxes. Emerging into the daylight once more, the hills beckon and quickly banish the consideration of either prospect.

The Black Mountains – Walk Five: Llanthony Priory and Garn Wen

Starting Point: Llanthony Priory – car park – toilets – picnic site.

Access: Easiest approach is from the well-signed road from the A465 at Llanvihangel Crucorney five miles north-east of Abergavenny.

Distance: 6¼ miles

Detail: Ascent of western slopes via Cwm Bwchel to Bal Bach and then to Garn Wen and Coed Ty Canol with return by woodland and field paths.

Map: 1:25,000 Outdoor Leisure Map No. 13.

The valley of the Honddu at Llanthony is but a narrow corridor between the mountains, with paths rising both east and west to provide superb viewpoints of the Priory in its setting. Two routes are described from this launching point which connect with other paths opening up possibilities for wider ranging circuits. Links to other walks in this book to provide expanded "horseshoe" routes for those who don't feel they have had a day out unless they have got a minimum of 15 miles and preferably 20 under their belt will readily suggest themselves to the owners of seven league boots.

The Walk

From the car park return past the elephant-grey ruins of the Priory and make your way back to the road. Turn left and take the path immediately on the right signed Bal Bach, passing The Mill with its `three horseshoes' name plate.

The path swings to the left to cross the Afon Honddu by a steel footbridge. Beyond the bridge turn right following the riverside edge of a short field. A further stile is crossed, then a trickle of a stream to a third stile. Here turn left, with the river on your right to meet and cross a wooden footbridge. Swing left over a soggy patch churned up by ponies and continue with the stream on your left.

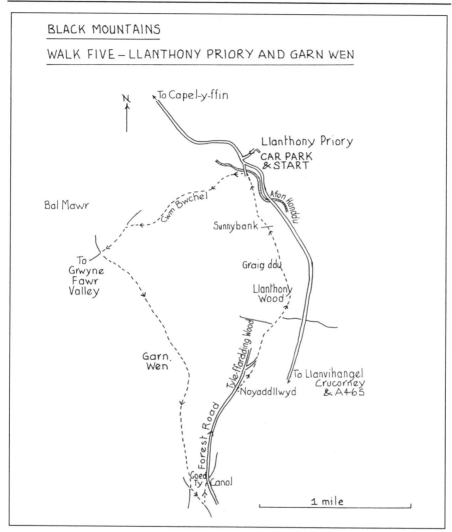

BLACK MOUNTAINS

WALK FIVE – LLANTHONY PRIORY AND GARN WEN

N

To Capel-y-ffin

Llanthony Priory

CAR PARK & START

Bal Mawr

Cwm Bwchel

Afon Honddu

Sunnybank

To Grwyne Fawr Valley

Graig ddu

Llanthony Wood

Garn Wen

Tyle-ffordding Wood

Forest Road

To Llanvihangel Crucorney & A465

Noyaddllwyd

Goed Ty Canol

1 mile

Pass through a metal gateway and head towards farm buildings in line with three trees rising up a gentle slope. At the third tree turn right to cross sleeper and turn left. In a few yards, cross a stile on your right and turn left. A short length of fenced path leads to yet another stile at the northern edge of the farm area; this is passed to your left, taking a track up the valley to a stile seen at the top corner of the field. Once over the stile, take a few steps left, then sharp right to follow the track which runs alongside a gully. Your direction has been roughly south of west and this is maintained as you climb to a further stile.

The long pull out of the valley provides widening views with the Priory occupying a proportionately smaller place in the landscape as it is dwarfed by the hills. To your left, the slopes drop down to the deep cleft of Cwm Bwchel through which the little stream flows under the privacy of the trees that mark its course.

The path continues to the head of the cwm on its northern side, the rim of the plateau seen ahead with bilberry and heather competing for a place with the bracken. Towards the head of the cwm a good track joins from diagonal right. A steady onward climb brings the summit of Bal Mawr (1992 ft) into view. The bracken has lost the battle for a place on the hillside, with heather and bilberry taking command. Here and there a patch of soft rush warns of wetter ground but the path is good and clear and should be followed until a large cairn marks a junction of paths.

To the right a path climbs to the summit of Bal Mawr but the interest is concentrated to the west and the Grwyne Fawr Valley. Here the Mynydd Du Forest spreads four miles up the centre of the blind valley, one and a half miles at its widest, with the topmost point crossing the 2500 ft contour close to Pen y Gadair Fawr. The forest having reached maturity has been part felled and replanted. Its disciplined climb up the mountain side, suggesting the precision of an architectural construction, faintly resembles a distant view of the Inca temples of Peru. An impression that may not occur to everybody and one not destined to last very long as the forest contours change with the increasing height of the new plantings.

Looking back to the east, the Priory has vanished from view but the long line of the ridge remains constant. To the south-east, the distinctive shape of Ysgyryd Fawr, the Holy Mountain, will be recognised by those already familiar with the topography of the area. A little further south, there is the wooded summit of its sister, Ysgyryd Fach. The sharp pimple erupting on the skyline at the southern end of the forest is the 1805 ft Crug Mawr, beyond which the Sugar Loaf makes its expected appearance.

From the cairn turn left, heading east of south on the clear path to the un-named higher ground reached in a quarter of a mile. From here maintain your direction on a long falling path with the cairn at Garn Wen seen ahead. Garn Wen literally translates to White Stones or White Cairn. Al-fred Watkins, the famous ley line hunter, in his intriguing book "The Old Straight Track", claims the cairn as a sighting mound for ancient travel-lers following the ridge paths.

Before the cairn is reached the path divides at a Y-junction, either will do, the right-hand fork taking a course close to the cairn but they eventually reunite.

As you draw level with the cairn, the red cliffs of Darren, which form the western scarp of Hatterrall Hill, are seen forward diago-nally left; they become increasingly prominent as a steady de-scent is made by the clear, bracken-edged path. Sugar Loaf, too, claims the attention with the eye leading down the Vale of Ewyas to Ysgyryd Fawr.

In a little under three-quarters of a mile from Garn Wen, the paths con-verge at the edge of Coed Ty Canol. Here continue with the wood to your left. When the trees fall back maintain your direction for 200 yards to a

Pony Trekkers above the Vale of Ewyas

cairn which marks a junction of paths. Here turn left and in a short distance swing half left on a falling path which provides a superb view up the Vale.

The right of way crosses a forest road and continues falling. Although overgrown in places, it cuts across the bottom edge of the wood, then northwards to exit by a stile and on to join the forest road which passes the farm at Noyaddllwyd. The forest road presents no such problems and its use is recommended – by courtesy of the forestry commission.

Emerging from the first block of forest – Coed Ty Canol – continue with the road for a short distance. When the gate is reached, do not pass through but go forward diagonally right, descending to a metal gateway. From here, a somewhat gloomy passage is made under the trees with the boundary of the wood on your left. At the end of the wood, pass through a gateway and on towards Upper Henllan. When the track to the farm is met bear left towards a gateway to ford a stream. Continue, rising through a hollow way which soon opens out to give views of the valley, albeit restricted. A wider track is met coming in from the left; go forward on this to pass through a gateway into Llanthony Wood.

The forest track divides after a quarter of a mile. Take the left, upper fork which soon passes the smartly-painted house of Graig-ddu. Continue on with the forest thinning out with the Priory and the summer cluster of tents at the camp site seen ahead. When the track makes a sharp hairpin bend to the right, leave it and take the narrower path to a gate which announces Sunnybank.

Just over 100 yards from Sunnybank, cross the stile on the right and head diagonally left over a field to the midway point of the next boundary. Keep the same (northerly) direction through the next field which is bisected by a farm track, then a further field to meet and cross a small stream with some assistance from stepping stones. Once over the water go ahead with the field boundary immediately to your left. At the end of the field exit by a stile and go forward to cross the steel footbridge over the Afon Honddu. Bear right up the narrow lane to the road, where you turn left and right to return to the car park.

The Black Mountains – Walk Six: Offa's Dyke Path and Loxidge Tump

Starting Point: Llanthony Priory picnic site.

Access: Leave the A465 at Llanvihangel Crucorney five miles north-east of Abergavenny taking the well-signed road. Llanthony is reached in 6 miles.

Distance: 5 miles.

Detail: A steady ascent to the ridge on the eastern side of the valley with good views, north along Offa's Dyke Path with a return over Loxidge Tump.

Map: 1:25,000 Outdoor Leisure Map No. 13.

Toilets: At picnic site.

This route provides excellent views from different angles of the Priory in its setting beneath the long mountain walls that all but enclose the narrow valley.

The Walk

From the car park walk back past the Priory and the church of St. David with its little bell turret and make for the five-barred gate and stile seen ahead. Beyond the stile, turn immediately right. When a further gate is reached, cross the stile and swing right, signed Longtown, with the Priory on your right – enclosed by a fine example of dry stone walling. As you reach the end of the wall cross a further stile and bear left up the hill with the field boundary on your left. (Note some maps may still show the right of way going diagonally over the field but clearly this path has now been sensibly re-routed). At the top of the field, turn right along the edge to reach the stile which leads into Wirral Wood.

Here is a good spot to pause and look around. Down the valley are the steep cliffs of Darren; to the west is the deep cleft of Cwm Bwchel which formed the outward leg of Walk Five, with Bal Mawr peeping over the edge of the plateau. The valley presents a

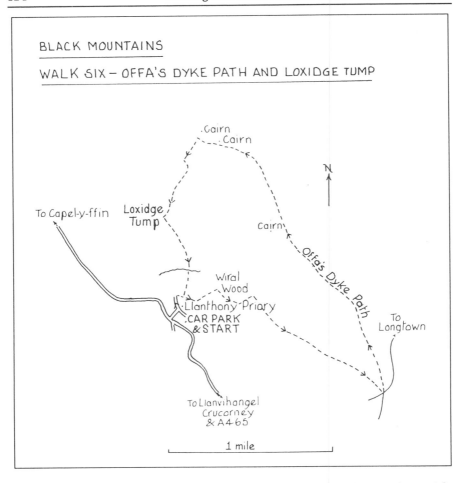

BLACK MOUNTAINS

WALK SIX – OFFA'S DYKE PATH AND LOXIDGE TUMP

superb picture of the ruined but elegant Priory in its setting with the land rising quickly beyond the band of field enclosures.

Take the rising eastward path through the woods which in 200 yards meets a metal gate. Cross the stile on the left which is found a few yards short of the gate. Take the steep path ahead. Ignore the first crossing path as shown on the OS map and 200 yards after leaving the wood cross a stile and turn right. (The path out of the valley has been waymarked but take care not to take the arrowed left turn at this point). A clear bracken-edged track is followed east of south through a semi-wooded area, with the fence line to your right.

Again there are views over the valley to the far hillside with its orderly forest plantations and the haphazard scatter of trees in na-

The Vale of Ewyas and Llanthony Priory from Loxidge Tump

ture's own garden. The track has been used to advantage by travellers long before twentieth-century leisure walkers set out to explore the hills and is also popular with pony trekkers. The leader of one group told me that the way, according to his grandfather, was used by the monks to collect beer from Longtown. That's turning the clock back some considerable time but not too far for the village has a long history with both castle ruins and the remains of a motte and bailey to prove it.

In just under a quarter of a mile, the track swings forward left, (south-east), climbing steeply away from the fence line at a point where some heart-shaped ponds are seen beyond the wall on the right.

The trees are left behind and the path takes a diagonal course bounded by bracken and the occasional clump of gorse. After half a mile, as the wood just below to your right comes to an end, a path will be noted swinging sharp left up the hillside; this is not our route but is useful to note for the future. Maintain your direction and in 500 yards gain the ridge top and Offa's Dyke Path.

At this point we leave the Longtown path but before turning left to pursue the ridge, it is worthwhile going forward a few yards to take a look over the farms of Herefordshire. When clouds scud along the ridges the landscape below can present an almost eerie appearance as the light plays strange tricks giving a semi-luminescence to the green fields and yellow stubble. An effect that is made the more sinister if a black garbed raven should happen to glide silently past as it hunts along the mist-wraithed edges. Local folklore may begin to assume a credibility not normally accorded to it at ground level. On such days, it has to be admitted that the old legend of a ghostly figure helping travellers lost on the hills is not so readily dismissed.

Rather than wait for him to come along with suitable directions, turn northwards, to follow the ridge for the next two miles. Here it is kinder underfoot, with few if any wet patches to dodge round, and the path runs clearly between heather and bilberry. In just over half a mile, a triangulation point is met, here the remains of small quarry pits may afford some minimal shelter from the wind for those pausing for rest and refreshment. A few steps to the right will again reveal "the promised land" of Herefordshire.

There is a change of direction from the trig point as the track now moves more west of north. After a short distance a line of cairns marks a path coming in from the left. Continue along the ridge with the occasional shooting butt or cairn dotting the way or indicating indistinct paths off the mountain.

As you advance along the ridge, Black Hill, explored in Walk One, comes into view (forward, right) and a useful little rock shelter is found by the path. As the widening plateau that nudges west to Loxidge Tump is approached, a small cairn marks paths both left and right, but continue to the larger cairn seen ahead. Map readers may like to note it is located on the 600 metre contour line and a little south of the spot height marked on the 1:25,000 as 605m and on the 1:50,000 as 604m. Here turn left, on an indistinct path which heads south-west over the gently falling plateau. There is a confusion of similarly faint sheep walks/paths – a compass bearing before setting off may be helpful until a landmark comes into view. Your line of travel should take you past the not very obvious cairn marked in gothic lettering on the map. The path broadens as you reach the rim of the plateau which offers fine views to the Priory and down the valley.

Bracken reappears as a stony path is followed to a "nose" jutting out from the hill. This is an excellent point from which to make a final survey of this delightful long valley embraced by the protective arms of the hills. A twisting path falls to pass under the little headland with your direction veering between the Priory and the white painted Half Moon Inn.

When the low walls of a ruined building are met by a clump of eight-feet-high box trees, continue with the path, swinging round in the direction of the Priory. Descend steeply passing through a gap in a stone wall to pick your way down to a wicket gate in the fence below the remains of an old quarry. From here, the path is waymarked.

Once through the gate, head downhill, crossing a rutted farm track and continue on to trees to a stile. Here pass through a narrow neck of woodland and over a further stile. Now diagonally right to the next boundary passing several dead but still standing sweet chestnut trees, their bare branches thrust out in supplication. Maintain your direction towards the Priory and beyond the metal gate and stile, bear half right. Cross a stream and exit by a stile to return to your starting point.

The Black Mountains – Walk Seven: Capel-y-ffin and Bal Mawr

Starting Point: Capel-y-ffin – no formal car park but there is space for a few cars on the verge beyond the bridge.

Access: Via the Vale of Ewyas – 3½ miles north of Llanthony or via the minor road from Hay-on-Wye – 2½ miles beyond Hay Bluff.

Distance: 8½ miles

Detail: Steep initial ascent, fine ridge walk and good views throughout.

Map: 1:25,000 Outdoor Leisure Map No. 13.

Each walk in the Black Mountains seems to be better than the last and this one certainly commands star rating, especially if taken in late August/early September when the heather is in full bloom. "Extras", which cannot be guaranteed, may include the sight of a fox lurking at the bracken edges, ravens gliding along the ridge, buzzards and other birds of prey. A special pleasure that may come your way as you pause on the steep climb to the plateau is an aerial view of a shepherd on horseback with his ever-obedient dogs, moving his flock on to pastures new. An unhurried but skilful manoeuvre that owes nothing to this bustling century, from which these hills provide so welcome an escape.

Capel-y-ffin must surely be well in the running for the title of Britain's smallest village. From the sign which announces your arrival only the tiny church, Chapel Farm and a barn can be immediately seen. A roving eye reveals a scatter of farms on the hillside, to which can be added the little group of buildings around the Grange Pony Trekking Centre and the Baptist Chapel. In summer the population must be more than doubled by the sudden mushrooming of a flush of green and white tents that dot the valley fields.

A dry stone wall and eight ancient yews enclose the churchyard of

St. Mary's: stone built, stone tiled and topped by a stumpy weather-boarded turret set at an almost jaunty angle. The time worn yews are surely older than the church which dates from the middle of the eighteenth century. Within, the church is scarcely bigger than a generously sized lounge with a gallery of passage width which provides a single a row of benches. The wooden pulpit bears an inscription noting that it was placed here in 1780. In recording the event it incidentally provides a memorial to the responsible church wardens, W. Bridgewater, D. Walker and its constructor K. Parry. The restoration of the church has added a finely engraved window – the words could scarcely be more apt in this setting – you might guess what it is: "I will lift up mine eyes unto the hills from whence cometh my help".

Gerald of Wales had noted the healthy benefits of residing in this valley and his opinion seems to be borne out by some of the headstones in the graveyard. On the wall by the porch William Williams of Neuadd is remembered "...who died Jan 28, 1776, age 90. Husband kind, a loving father, a neighbour mild".

A short distance up the lane and over the brook, is the white-painted Baptist chapel. It is not open for inspection, but a plaque records that William and David Prosser brought the ministry of the gospel to their house in the year 1737: "...Mr John Griffiths secured the sum of one hundred pounds for the use of the ministry for the time being, died June 29 1817...".

It was to this remote valley that the Rev. Joseph Leycester Lyne came in 1869 to establish his monastery on the hillside. Lyne was a man out of the ordinary mould, some would no doubt have called him an eccentric, others a mystic, a visionary, others a rebel. Certainly he was in conflict with the church authorities for views which were regarded as extreme. His ordination in 1860 as a deacon of the Church of England went ahead only on the understanding that he would refrain from preaching for a period of three years. By 1862, he had adopted the style of Father Ignatius and it is by this name that he is best known.

The monastery was duly built and work started on a never-to-be-completed chapel, where he now lies buried in the roof-

Capel-y-ffin beneath Darren Lwyd.

less chancel. He seems to have been a speaker of great ability, commanding a ready audience both in this country and on an evangelizing visit to North America in 1890. Long after his death in 1908 he is still remembered and news letters are periodically issued by the Father Ignatious Memorial Trust.

Eric Gill, sculptor and typographer, settled at the monastery with other artists and writers during the nineteen thirties and a tablet commemorating his time here ends with the words "My work is my leisure, my leisure my work". Printers will know Gill for the design of type faces that are still in use, of which perhaps the best known is Gill Sans-serif.

Monastery and chapel ruins are open to the public and can be visited by a short diversion from the walk.

The Walk

As you face Capel-y-ffin from the Llanthony approach take the rising lane on the left signed to the Grange Pony Trekking Centre. Soon the white painted monastery will be seen on the left and the tall grey skeleton of the chapel. A quarter of a mile from the village, turn left on the narrow lane which divides in a hundred yards. A wayside memorial to Father Ignatius is found on the right with the inscription "Peace to the wayfarer through the blood of Jesus".

The left fork leads to the monastery where visitors are welcome to inspect the non-denominational chapel under the rafters of the upper floor. A few steps beyond the monastery buildings lies the half completed chapel, also open for inspection. Father Ignatius chose the site well, for there is a splendid view to the hills that enclose Capel-y-ffin, surely inspirational to those of a religious or artistic persuasion. A statue of the Virgin Mary, looks not to the hills but to the approaching visitor.

Retrace your steps to the lane and continue uphill passing the white painted, virginia creeper-covered Grange. The track soon reaches the gate to the open hillside.

From the gate take a few steps to your right then immediately left on a track, much worn by the passage of pony trekkers. This takes a zig-zag course up the hillside, bringing you within sixty yards of the top end of a fir plantation. The path now curves to the right and becomes grassy un-

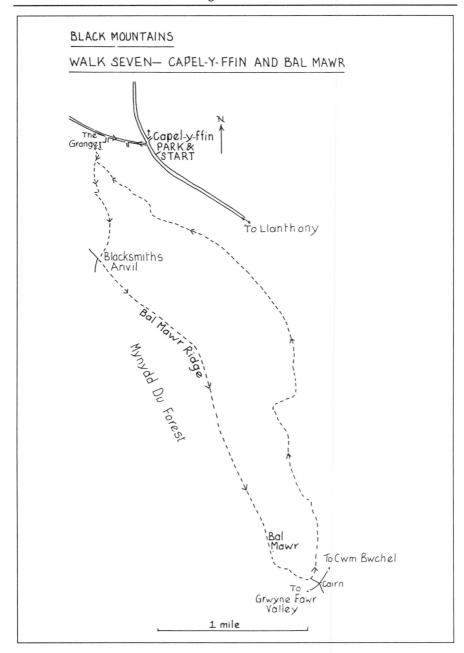

BLACK MOUNTAINS

WALK SEVEN— CAPEL-Y-FFIN AND BAL MAWR

1 mile

der-foot and in a few paces swings left. Your direction is now generally south, advancing over a level(ish) patch of land to cross a stony bottomed stream.

Beyond the stream make for the path that can be clearly seen as it climbs the mountain wall. A long steep zig-zag ascent which provides spectacular views.

Capel-y-ffin, never large, is but a dot on the landscape. The prospect to the north up the valley towards the dip between Twmpa and Rhos Dirion is particularly fine and reminiscent of the northern Pennines. Overall the mountains are seen in all their splendour, gracefully curved contours carrying to the almost flat-topped summit ridges. The slopes are clad in a multitude of greens which shade to beige then brown as summer advances into autumn.

The path becomes less distinct as the cliff gives way to less steep slopes and swings west of south. A series of cairns will bring you to the main path which runs along the centre of the ridge which is itself marked by a cairn of generous proportions. From here the dam which holds in check the waters of the Grwyne Fawr Reservoir will be seen to your right. To the west lies the shapely summit of Pen y Gadair Fawr, always a useful landmark.

Turn left, (south-east) taking the path to the final ridge which, in just over half a mile, peaks at 2227 ft by a scatter of stones, the debris of an abandoned quarry. From here the ridge, which resembles the keel of an upturned boat, runs for a mile and a quarter to the triangulation point on Bal Mawr. Level walking at first, then a gradual descent with expansive views.

To the right the Mynydd du Forest, nearly four miles long, climbs both sides of the Grwyne Fawr Valley, its dusty roads white arteries snaking through the forest green. To the left the sharp ridge of Black Hill is seen as it rises to join the main body of the mountains a mile or so short of Hay Bluff. Sugar Loaf is forward, half-right, balanced by Ysgyryd Fawr more to the east. This high moorland is seen at its best in late summer with a purple carpet rolled out over the hills.

As the end of the ridge is approached, Llanthony Priory is briefly seen far below and from the triangulation point the Garn Wen cairn is but a distant black silhouette. The way now falls toward the crossroads of paths that meet at the top of the pass; this crosses the hills from Llanthony by way of Cwm Bwchel with the intersection marked by a large cairn.

About 100 yards short of the cairn swing left to head north on a narrow but clear path, the junction marked by a steel post. (Note the second steel post, not an earlier one which may have been noted a little below the summit of Bal Mawr).

The generally level track improves as progress is made and is followed under the flanks of the Bal Mawr ridge, but above the Vale of Ewyas, for just over a mile before any appreciable change of direction is made. A ravine in the hillside is rounded, followed by a small cleft by a pair of ruined buildings. From here there is a fine view down the valley with Llanthony Priory all but lost in the broad canvas.

The heather has been replaced by bracken, with the falling path now swinging northwards. In a quarter of a mile, a path is seen rising from the right by the fence line; go ahead (still north) passing through a metal gateway. The path narrows, passes a ruined building and exits from the enclosed land by a further metal gateway.

Continue with the track, keeping the fence line when it appears to your right until, in about a mile and a half, a marshy walled area is met and passed on your left. Beyond the path climbs with a wire fence and ruined wall to your right with a view to Darren Lwyd and the Gospel Pass. At the top of the rise the fence falls back a little, continue on for just over a quarter of a mile. As you draw level with the fir plantation which lies above the Grange, cross a stream and bear a little to the right, then follow the zig-zag path of your outward journey to descend to the gate. From here head downhill, passing the Grange to the metalled lane, where you turn right to return to Capel-y-ffin.

The Black Mountains – Walk Eight: Grwyne Fawr and the Northern Escarpment

Starting Point: Blaen-y-cwm car park.

Access: Leave the A465 at Llanvihangel Crucorney and follow the Llanthony road as far as Stanton where you turn left i.e. second left after passing under the railway bridge. In a mile and three-quarters, at the Five Ways crossroads, turn right signed Grwyne Fawr Reservoir. Follow the valley road for six miles. Ignore the first forest car park and carry on to Blaen-y-cwm near the northern end of the Mynydd Du Forest.

Distance: 8 miles.

Detail: A steady ascent to the ridge is followed by a long passage over open moorland to fine views from the northern escarpment. Thence return by falling path passing the reservoir.

Map: 1:25,000 Outdoor Leisure Map No. 13.

Grwyne Fawr is a long, remote and beautifully green valley – a no through road so far as the motorist is concerned, but the track that climbs the northern scarp via Rhiw Cwnstab provides an excellent highway for the walker with useful links to other paths. Geraldis in his twelfth century "Journey through Wales" estimated that its sister valley, the Vale of Ewyas, was but three bow shots wide. Had the scribe used the same unit of measurement in Grwyne Fawr, he might have found that at the point where our walk starts, he would only have had need of a single arrow, for the forested hills rise immediately from the road.

The Walk

From the southern end of the car park take the northward track which returns to the road. Shortly it joins another track which soon divides where take the diagonally right track which rises to join a forest road. In a short distance, abandon the road as it takes a sharp turn to the right. Take the narrow path northwards which in just over 300 yards leaves the forest by a gate to emerge onto the open moorland.

Looking up the valley, the wall of the dam can be seen, the opposite ridge shows the forest climbing up to but not overcoming the 2625 ft Pen y Gadair Fawr. This shapely summit is rather more impressive than its slightly taller brother Waun Fach, a little to the north; at 2660 ft, the latter can claim to be King of the Black Mountains if height is the only criterion of sovereignty.

From the gate, maintain your northerly direction on a not too clear path seen in the bracken ahead. The way to the summit ridge is indistinct and confusion is added by the appearance of several sheep walks or faint paths. The bridle path which is the way over the hills to Capel-y-ffin should take you to a large cairn where turn left, (north) on the distinct ridge top track. Theory and practice may diverge, so you may hit the ridge a little further to the north than intended; no matter, as long as you climb at an angle to the slope you will eventually strike the ridge path. If your passage has taken you just above the second stream shown on the map you are well on course and from here swing a little to the right.

There now follows a three and a half mile north-easterly trek to the triangulation point at the top of the escarpment. The way is punctuated by several boundary stones bearing large, clear but enigmatic initials or fading inscriptions and several cairns. It is a good grassy path providing comfortable walking, a further glimpse of the dam on the left and the slopes of Darren Lwyd on the right. After two and a half miles, 300 feet of height will have been added as Twyn Talycefn (2303 ft) is reached. At its northern end, four boundary stones are set together in a tight square; at least, that was the intention – for one has now fallen. H and B are the legends on one, the others which once carried rather more information are not readily decipherable.

Just beyond this point the path divides at a Y-junction. (The right curving path heads over Rhos Dirion). Take the left (forward) fork which, in just under three-quarters of a mile, will bring you to the triangulation point (2339 ft) on Pen Rhos Dirion, the turning point of the next leg of the walk.

The view from the survey station is restricted, so go forward a short distance to the scarp edge for an expansive prospect of the Wye Valley. Immediately below is a network of paths crisscross-

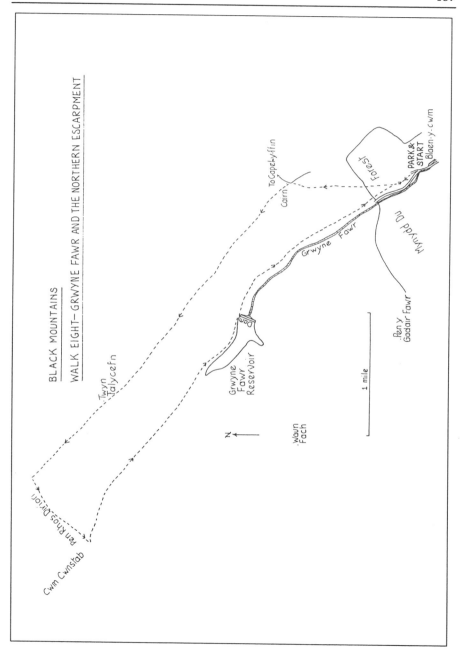

BLACK MOUNTAINS

WALK EIGHT— GRWYNE FAWR AND THE NORTHERN ESCARPMENT

To Capel-y-ffin

Cairn

Grwyne Fawr

Forest

PARK &
START
Blaen-y-cwm

Mynydd Du

Pen y
Gadair Fawr

Twyn
Talycefn

Grwyne
Fawr
Reservoir

Dam

Waun
Fach

N

1 mile

Pen Rhos Dirion

Cwm Cwnstab

ing the bracken covered area. Beyond lies a great mosaic of field enclosures which climb steadily to the higher ground. A wide arc of hills includes the Radnor Forest. Hay-on-Wye is hidden but a glimpse of the silvered thread of the river may be seen. Looking right along the edge, Lord Hereford's Knob obscures most of Hay Bluff. To the left, (south-west) the Brecon Beacons loom darkly, twelve miles distant if measured by the proverbial flight of the crow.

Retrace your steps to the triangulation point taking the clear but sometimes soggy south-westerly path a little away from the scarp edge. In three-quarters of a mile, cairns mark a junction of paths at the top of the

Grwyne Fawr valley looking to the Pen y Gadair ridge.

deep cleft of Cwm Cwnstab. Here turn left, south-east, on a well-worn path which soon recovers its grassy surface. In half a mile, a stream, the Blaen Grwyne Fawr, is crossed.

From here, the path parallels the course of the stream as it digs itself deeper and deeper into the cleft of the valley descending with the aid of a succession of mini waterfalls. The path, classified as "Road used as a public path" has no such inhibitions and keeps well above it. In a mile, the unfettered progress of the stream is arrested as it supplies the half-mile-long Grwyne Fawr Reservoir – condemned to a never-ending task of filling a bottomless bucket. Some reservoirs soon blend into the landscape, but not this one for its sharply-cut slopes will always proclaim its man-made origin, even when the dam with its central church-like tower is not visible.

Beyond the dam the track becomes wider falling steadily for a mile and a half to reach the forest edge and the road which will return you to the car park.

The Black Mountains – Walk Nine: Grwyne Fawr and the Bal Mawr Ridge

Starting Point: Forestry Commission's Blaen-y-cwm car park.

Access: Leave A465 at Llanvihangel Crucorney and follow the Llanthony road as far as Stanton where turn left – i.e. second left after passing under the railway bridge. Turn right at Five Ways signed to Grwyne Fawr Reservoir. Follow the valley road for six miles with Blaen-y-cwm car park located near the northern end of the Mynydd Du Forest.

Distance: 6¼ miles.

Detail: After an initial climb through the forest a period of level walking gives good views which expand as the Bal Mawr ridge is followed northwards.

Maps: 1:25,000 Outdoor Leisure Map No. 13.

The pleasant Grwyne Fawr valley and the airy Bal Mawr ridge are too good to be dismissed with only a single visit. The upper valley and the reservoir has already been explored on the return leg from the northern escarpment on Walk Eight. The long Bal Mawr ridge which provides such a superb view point was followed north to south in the route from Capel-y-ffin described in Walk Seven. This walk traverses the ridge in the opposite direction with a gradual unfolding of the northern landscape as progress is made.

The Walk

Park at the southern end of the car park and then retrace your steps down the valley road for a short distance. Immediately after passing a cottage take the path on the left signed Llanthony. The general direction of travel for the next mile and a half is east of south.

At first, the path runs between a stream to your right and a stone wall to your left. After a short distance, it swings diagonally left up the hillside to meet and cross a forest road. Take the signed path ahead and continue

BLACK MOUNTAINS

WALK NINE – GRWYNE FAWR AND THE BAL MAWR RIDGE

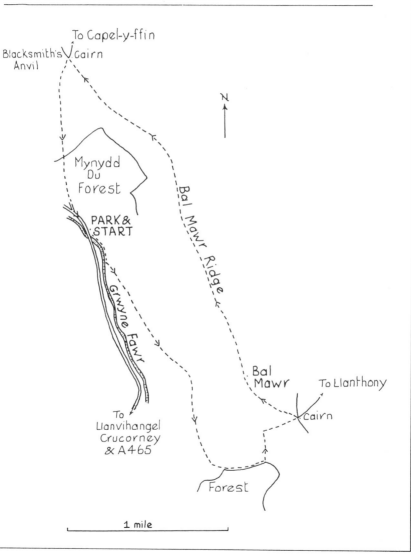

To Capel-y-ffin

Blacksmith's Anvil

Cairn

N

Mynydd Du Forest

PARK & START

Bal Mawr Ridge

Grwyne Fawr

Bal Mawr

To Llanthony

Cairn

To Llanvihangel Crucorney & A465

Forest

1 mile

climbing, soon to meet and follow a stone wall to your right. The skeleton of a stone building is passed, and then a second, beyond which a further forest road is met. Cross the road and take the narrow path almost immediately opposite which briefly plunges into the deep gloom of closely packed trees.

The trees thin out and the path runs through bracken to reach a fence and waymarked stile. Here turn half left and, in summer at least, you will be walking through thick bracken. The path reveals itself as you advance and provides improving views to the forest across the valley to your right.

A further fence with a stile is met with a waymark pointing directly ahead. The bracken is now much reduced and the grassy path continues to cross a small, rocky bedded stream; it veers a little to the left to cross a further trickle by yet another ruin and continues to a gateway at the edge of the open hillside.

From the gateway cross a field of rough grass and a generous crop of thistle passing a derelict stone building to reach a metal gate and stile set by a stone wall. Beyond the stile go forward slight diagonally left on an indistinct path which in about 150 yards joins a broad grassy track running north/south.

Turn right with the track which contours the hillside, springy under foot and with excellent views, northwards to the upper valley of Grwyne Fawr and southwards with the summit of Sugar Loaf in the distance. The western view is dominated by the huge expanse of the forest and to the east the high and inviting Bal Mawr ridge.

The track is followed for just under three-quarters of a mile to a boundary wall, where it veers to the left. Continue with the track for a further quarter of a mile with the wall/fence line immediately to your right until a metal gateway is encountered on your right where a broad track leaves the forested area.

Turn left, up the bank, joining a clear track through bracken maintaining your direction roughly northwards for just under 300 yards. (To put a little more detail on this – when a crossing path is met, turn left for a few yards and cross a minor stream and continue on with the path broadening and still climbing). The path divides after a short distance beyond the stream; take the right fork, heading north of east on a rising, narrow, but clear path through a mix of heather, bilberry and stunted bracken. In 600 yards, the path delivers you to a large cairn marking a junction of paths, the turning point of Walk Five from Llanthony and Walk Seven from Capel-y-ffin.

This is a good spot to take in the geography of walking in this part of the Black Mountains if you are not already familiar with the terrain. To the south a track climbs to higher ground before continuing on over the moorland to Garn Wen. To the north-east the broad track descends to Llanthony by Cwm Bechel, to the south-west a path falls to the forest. In the immediate area there is a choice of tracks heading north passing at different levels under the eastern flanks of Bal Mawr towards Capel-y-ffin. Our own route lies directly to the summit of Bal Mawr. This is a natural spot to pause and enjoy the scene which includes the great expanse of the forest and the long ridge to the east that carries the Offa's Dyke Path above Llanthony, although the tiny village and the Priory are absent from view. An all-round pleasing prospect which is greatly enhanced by the ridge walk.

From the cairn turn northwards on the clear rising track to Bal Mawr, which as it steepens has become eroded. The extra height gives a fine view of the rolling heather moorland, purpled in autumn and the greener landscape of the lower slopes of the hills above Llanthony. The path eases to reach the triangulation point, a little under 2000 ft. Now the Mynydd Du Forest is laid out for inspection, a giant relief map with the tabled topped Pen y Gadair Fawr at its northern end.

Head up the ridge, with a long and improving view up the Grwyne Fawr Valley with the distant dam wall increasingly visible but still only a small component of the landscape. To your right a backward glance will eventually reveal Llanthony and its Priory, an even smaller feature in the widening prospect.

A mile and a half of steady walking brings you to the highest point on the ridge, 2227 ft, marked by a handsome cairn constructed from the spoil of abandoned quarries.

The northward view now includes the Gospel Pass to Hay Bluff and the Darren Lwyd ridge leading on to Twmpa and our own "spine" falling and widening from ridge to plateau, before climbing to terminate on the scarp edge of Pen Rhos Dirion. In the far distance to the right will be seen the long shadowy grey outline of the nine-mile run of the Malvern Hills and, nearer at hand, the Vision Farm tucked under the hill near Capel-y-ffin.

Darren Lwyd Ridge, the Gospel Pass and Hatterall Ridge from Bal Mawr ridge.

The path continues forward, falling to the hump of the Blacksmith's Anvil and to the prominent cairn that marks yet another crossroad of paths. (Not too obvious a meeting of the ways for the paths are indistinct). To the right lies the way to the edge of the ridge and a steep descent to Capel-y-ffin. Our route turns left, heading initially in the direction of Pen y Gadair Fawr over grassy falling ground with a labyrinth of sheep walks and promising looking paths that fade away.

The direction of travel quickly swings south and you must take your pick of the paths which appear. Precise instruction is impossible except to indicate that a steady southern descent of half a mile, at an angle to the ridge you have just left, will bring you to the forest edge. There are two gates in the forest boundary, the first by a more mature plantation meets a forest road about a quarter of a mile from its northern apex. If you hit this gate first, ignore it and continue along the outside of the fence descending for 150 yards to the second gate which should be marked with a blue bridleway arrow.

Beyond the gate descend half diagonally right for 300 yards to a forest road at a wide bend. Here, turn right and, in a little under 100 yards, take the narrower falling path on the right. The path descends to a track coming in from the right, where go forward left. This leads down to the road, turn left and in a few yards take the track on the left which will return you to the southern end of the parking area.

The Black Mountains – Walk Ten: Y Grib and Waun Fach

Starting Point: Dinas car park.

Access: Three miles south of Talgarth via A479. Turn left at Pengenffordd on a single track road to reach the layby car park in a quarter of a mile.

Distance: 8½ miles.

Detail: Long and steady ascent of Y Grib provides excellent views to the north. From Y Das a passage over grassy moorland leads to Waun Fach the highest point of the Black Mountains – can be wet underfoot.

Maps: 1:25,000 Outdoor Leisure Map No. 13.

On a clear day, this route offers one of the most expansive views over the Wye Valley. After visiting the highest of the Black Mountains, a view is revealed down to the most remote of the valleys – Grwyne Fechan. The roadside parking spot lies under the northern slopes of Castell Dinas, an Iron Age fort in a commanding position above the Crickhowell/Talgarth road. The military value of this site overlooking a natural line of travel was not lost on the Normans who built a motte and bailey within the area. The Outdoor Leisure Map shows the permitted paths which give access and a diversion to the fort is included on the return leg of the walk that follows.

The pass makes the true boundary of the Black Mountains with the hills to the west that are outside the scope of this book. The 1476 ft summit that carries the fort signals the start of the six-mile, as the crow flies, northern wall of the Black Mountains, linking the ridges which have been explored in preceding pages.

The Walk

From the car park, from which there are already good views over the Wye Valley, go forward to take the public footpath signposted half-right. A good broad track passes Dinas Farm to your left and, as it climbs, on the right there is a view of the pointed northern summit of Mynydd Troed which only just fails to reach 2000 ft; the addition of the Ordnance Survey's triangulation point probably remedies this situation!

As you near the top of the rise swing left with the track to meet and pass through a metal gateway. With fence and a broken stone wall to your left, follow the wide track north-east along the flanks of the hills: a level way set at 1250 ft with a wide view beyond the Wye Valley, including the Radnor Forest with the 2132 ft Black Mixen identified by the thin thread of the wireless mast twenty miles to the north.

A backward glance reveals the distant profiles of the Brecon Beacons beyond which lies the dark shadow of the Black Mountain. To your right, the view is blocked by the continuous mountain wall which, as progress is made, reveals the rocky summit of Y Grib. Ahead lies Mynydd Bychan, a spur jutting out from the main mass of the hills which, together with Y Grib, cradles the deep Cwm y Nant where a score of springs tumble through deep ravines.

From the gate the track runs for a full half mile to reach a narrow lane where a public footpath is signed up the hillside. There is no need to continue to the road for, about 250 yards short of it, just as the track begins to fall to meet it, take the broad rutted track which heads diagonally right towards the cwm. Cross the deep cleft made by a stream and continue towards the fence line.

As you near the fence, swing diagonally right up the hillside, heading roughly eastwards. A steady climb of over half a mile on a good track takes you over the shoulder of Y Grib, marked by a cairn, to reach the plateau by a further cairn. Continue with the broad track, swinging left, i.e. north-east, following the scarp edge overlooking the immensely impressive scoop of Cwm y Nant.

Here the views to the Wye Valley and the distant hills of what used to be Radnorshire, the border county of north-west Herefordshire and through to Shropshire fuse together in a great arc. There are glimpses also of Myndd Troed and the Beacons. In the foreground, a green field is broken by a splash of white, identifying the airfield from which the gliding club sends forth its adventurers in search of the thermals which the buzzards already

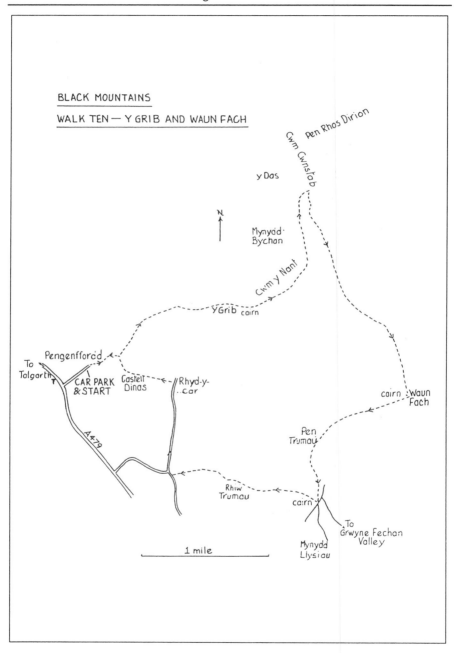

Northern escarpment ascending Y Grib.

ride so easily. You in your turn can look down upon the birds, always a satisfying experience for the hill walker.

About half-way along the ellipse of the scarp that leads towards Mynydd Bychan, an obvious cairn is seen. If time permits, turn right over the plateau for a short distance to view the steep drop from the spur that runs between Waun Fach and Pen Trumau.

Retracing your steps to the path, continue with the track leaving the spurs of Mynydd Bychan and Y Das on your left (separated by the cleft of Cwm Dwr-y-coed). Our way is heading towards, but stops short of, the junction of a number of mountain tracks marked by several cairns at the top of Rhiw Cwnstab.

The paths run as follows: Ahead – north-east – to the triangulation point on Pen Rhos Dirion, (Walk Eight) and thence in a further mile and a quarter to Lord Hereford's Knob, before descending to the Gospel pass. To the south-east a good track rounds down to the Grwyne Fawr Valley (also Walk Eight)) and to the left, north, descends to the foot of the scarp via Rhiw Cwnstab.

Our own route runs off about 200 yards short of this junction, taking a distinct track to the right, south, over grassy moorland. The steadily rising track is followed for a mile and three-quarters, over Pen y Manllwyn and on to Waun Fach which at 2660 ft is the highest point of the Black Mountains.

In a dry summer the way is soft and springy under-foot, a pleasure to walk, but in a wet season some dodging around soggy patches may be necessary. The width of the plateau forbids views to the Grwyne Fawr Valley from the path, but the ridge tops to the east will be picked out and identified by those who have followed earlier walks. Evidence of mans presence here long ago is indicated, at least on the map, by a hut circle, some way short of Pen y Manllwyn.

A short diversion to the right when you reach the cairn on Pen y Manllwyn provides good views, particularly a closer look to the steep fall from the spur to Pen Trumau.

Waun Fach, King of the Black Mountains, by virtue of its height, is not impressive when approached by this track from the north. It presents a vastly superior image when viewed from the west as will shortly be discovered. As you reach the summit plateau, a large concrete base is met; turn right (west) as directed by the red arrow. A wide track runs along the top of the spur, losing a little height as it curves towards the south-west to reach the sharp nose of Pen Trumau. (Note: a cairn part way along the ridge marks the way, when the path divides just beyond this take the left fork).

A small rocky platform on Pen Trumau provides not only the promised improved image of Waun Fach but to Pen y Gadair Fawr and a long view down the Grwyne Fechan valley.

A short descent is now made to the saddle between Pen Trumau and Mynydd Llysiau where a cairn marks a further junction of paths.

The excellence of the path from the Grwyne Fechan Valley which has terraced the eastern slope of Mynydd Llysiau is worth noting for future reference and is used in subsequent walks.

From the cairn turn immediately right, north-west, in 200 yards the path divides, ignore the right fork. The good, always clear, path heads generally westwards, curving a little to the right as it descends to reach the fence line in three-quarters of a mile.

The enclosed land of the valley is met by a metal gate, and in a few yards a further gateway. Beyond this, the track continues westwards between fences and on through a green tunnel to a minor road.

Turn right up the lane, ignoring the left turn, and continuing with the signed No Through Road for three-quarters of mile, just beyond the farm at Rhyd-y-car. After crossing a stream take the track on the left by a small grassy triangle. Head up the hedged path soon with a deep hollow created by a streamlet. It is easier to walk up this rather than trying to keep your footing on the greasy sides of the track.

Continue through a series of metal gateways with the quality of the path eventually improving. In a little under half a mile after leaving the road, the track swings to the right, climbing through a cutting. A short distance beyond the top of the rise a stile on the left leads to the permissive path for the diversion to Castell Dinas mentioned at the beginning of the walk.

Beyond the stile a field is crossed and then a steepening climb to the fort with its deeply ditched defences and the remains of a Norman motte and bailey.

The fort is a superb viewpoint including Mynydd Troed, a wide sweep of the Wye Valley, the outward section of the walk toward Y Das, the upper Rhiangoll Valley under Y Grib, Waun Fach and beyond to the long Pen Allt Mawr ridge.

Retrace your steps back to the stile and turn left. In 60 paces go through a metal gateway and swing left on the broad stony track which after passing Dinas Farm on your right will return you to your starting point.

The Black Mountains – Walk Eleven: Grwyne Fechan Valley and Mynydd Llysiau

Starting Point: Small car park on the minor road near Neuadd Fawr.

Access: Leave Crickhowell on the road signed to Llanbedr and follow it northward for 3 miles ignoring the turn to Llanbedr. The small car park is located just beyond the bridge over a stream at a sharp loop in the lane and about a quarter of a mile from the farm at Neuadd Fawr.

Distance: 9½miles.

Detail: A steady climb from the Hermitage follows the Grwyne Fechan Valley then rises sharply to Mynydd Llysiau with a 3-mile traverse of the ridge via Pen Twyn Glas.

Map: 1:25,000 Outdoor Leisure Map No 13.

Crickhowell is an attractive town on the River Usk spanned by an ancient 13-arched bridge. A town walk leaflet published by the Brecon Beacons National Park Committee describes many of its interesting buildings and tells something of its past history. The white walled, grey tiled Bridge End Inn is worthy of mention for its impressive display of hanging baskets and window boxes. The ruins of Alisby's Castle remain as a reminder of less peaceful times and the inns of the "romantic" age of coach travel. Wherever you look your eye is inevitably led to the hills, with the shapely Table Mountain and its Iron Age fort looking over the town from the north. Several paths off the minor road to Llanbedr are signed to Table Mountain but space to leave cars is limited. The second Crickhowell walk includes a diversion to Table Mountain in the course of a longer expedition.

Sir George Everest, Surveyor General of India, lived nearby and has the distinction of having the world's highest mountain named after him. Just off the Talgarth road, (A479) Tretower Castle and Court, now in the care of the Welsh Historic Monuments is open to the public. The tower dates from shortly after the Norman conquest with the later addition of a fortified house, home of the Picard, Herbert and Vaughan families over many centuries.

The long steady climb along the flanks of the hill above the Grwyne Fechan valley is a particularly enjoyable feature of this walk. The easy to follow path is also a very useful return route for other excursions in the area.

The Walk

The parking place is the last practical spot to leave a car but the lane must be pursued for a further mile and a half. This lengthy stretch of road is no hardship, since it provides very pleasant walking and fine views of the hills that surround this remote valley. In just under a mile the road makes a sharp right turn by the entrance to Cwm Farm. **Ignore this change of direction** and continue with the lane despite the No Through Road sign. Squirrels are particularly active along this section, raiding the hedgerows for the autumn crop of hazel nuts. The road narrows after a while and is signed Tal-y-maes Bridge. When a gate is met with the legends "Tal-y-maes Farm" and "Private Road – No Vehicles", continue on to Hermitage Bridge.

To the right are the remains of the house after which the bridge is named. Despite the ecclesiastical nomenclature it apparently had no religious connections – its remote situation being more than sufficient justification for its name.

A little beyond the bridge the road divides, take the left fork, a stony track which climbs through woodland with the stream, the Grwyne Fechan below to your left. The trees soon fall back and as the walk progresses views open up to give a long prospect of the hills ahead. To your left, the long ridge of the Mynydd Llysiau, which forms the return route effectively walls in the valley.

Six hundred yards from Hermitage Bridge the metalled track is abandoned as it swings right to Tal-y-maes Farm. Maintain your north-westerly direction on a wide grassy track which leads through a gate with improving views. The track descends to a further gate and then crosses

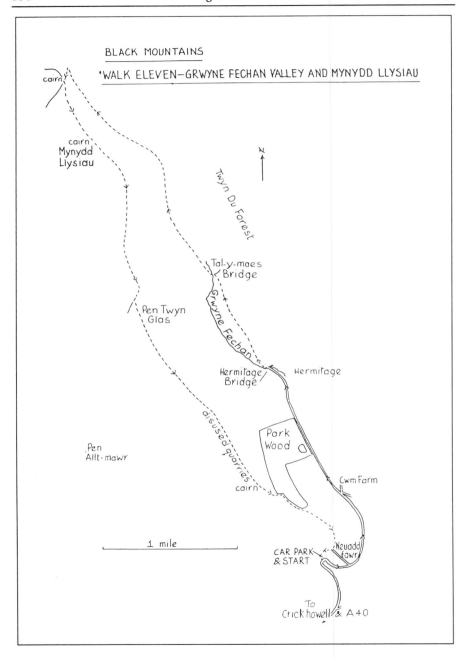

BLACK MOUNTAINS

'WALK ELEVEN—GRWYNE FECHAN VALLEY AND MYNYDD LLYSIAU

cairn

cairn
Mynydd
Llysiau

Twyn Du Forest

N

Tal-y-maes
Bridge

Grwyne Fechan

Pen Twyn
Glas

Hermitage
Bridge

Hermitage

disused quarries

Park
Wood

Pen
Allt-mawr

Cwm Farm

cairn

1 mile

Neuadd
fawr

CAR PARK
& START

To
Crickhowell & A40

Tal-y-maes bridge.

the single arched stone bridge over the Grwyne Fechan – a delightful spot with a small waterfall a short way upstream.

Beyond the bridge, swing right on the clear path climbing steadily north-westerly along the flanks of the hill. This is an excellent path, an easy gradient, soft and springy underfoot.

The Twyn Du Forest climbs the slopes above the river to your right. Peny y Gadair Fawr just tipping over Gadair Fawr and further to the north Waun Fach, the Black Mountains highest point falls sharply away from its soggy plateau. This section of the map is noticeably blue-veined, with web after web of streams falling down the steep slopes of the moorland, more than you will see in any other part of the Black Mountains.

The track continues beside a fence set on the remains of an old stone wall. As this comes to an end, veer to the left as you climb deep into the heart of the mountains with the spur from Waun Fach to Pen Tramau directly ahead. The hills gradually close in with the track turning sharp left to climb to the cairn which marks the crossroad of paths on the saddle between Pen Tramau and Mynydd Llysiau.

Here the westward prospect which has been hidden by the great mass of the Mynydd Llysiau ridge opens up. First, the falling view to the Rhiangoll Valley dominated from here by Mynydd Troed, then onwards to the Brecon Beacons and in the far distance the Black Mountains.

At the cairn turn left (south), to make the short sharp climb to the northern end of Mynydd Llysiau the extra height giving an even wider prospect. Waun Fach and Pen y Gadair to be admired again, and the Beacons coming in more strongly.

There is now a steady three-mile walk southwards along the ridge, at its highest 2175 ft. Initially there is a good view down to the Grwyne Fechan Valley with sheep grazing far below, a small white sailed armada dotted over a green sea. The view to the Beacons and the Black Mountain is retained rather longer. Pen Allt-mawr, 2359 ft, is seen forward half right; the topmost tip of the Mynydd du Forest appears by Pen y Gadair and the ubiquitous Sugar Loaf is seen ahead as you continue southwards to Pen Twyn Glas, 2119 ft. Note: From the Pen Trumau saddle to Pen Twyn Glas, it is one and three-quarter miles with a further one and a half miles to the end of the ridge.

Cairns mark the way at intervals and a series of boundary stones will be encountered close to the track. Worn by wind and weather some are difficult to read, others have fallen but the legends variously proclaim ownership by Mrs McNamara; Tretower M; Sir J Bailey, Bart.

Just short of Pen Twyn Glas, the path divides; keep to the left fork. From Pen Twyn Glas the path gradually descends eventually to pass through a tumble of rocks, the debris of past quarrying activities. Here a decision on which of several paths to take is resolved by heading directly to the large cairn seen ahead at the far end of the ridge.

The views to the Beacons have long been blocked out as Pen Allt-mawr leads on to Pen Cerrig-calch. Dark, brooding and slightly menacing when the light is behind them, their gloom relieved by the wooded Cwm Banw above which buzzards soar with enviable ease.

From the cairn take the path forward left which falls to a track in about 100 yards. Bear left with this dropping down towards a stone wall and stile. Once over the stile follow the outside edge of the forest on a falling track, swing left with it after a short distance.

When the forest boundary falls back sharply (eastwards) maintain your south-easterly direction over a field for a quarter of a mile. A gradual descent towards closing stone walls which funnel you through a gateway, beyond which continue descending through a hollow way. About a quarter of a mile from the gate the track swings sharp left. At this point a permissive path is signposted to the right with a generous collection of white arrow waymarks which will quickly return you to your starting point thus: From the angle of the track go right over a stile and forward for forty paces, then sharp left down the steep slope towards the stream and in 100 yards by a large oak swing left to return to the car park by a stile.

After rain, the unsuspected presence of a small waterfall behind the car park may be revealed and I am told that both trout and salmon travel on from the Usk to spawn in the stream that runs through Cwm Banw.

The Black Mountains – Walk Twelve:
Table Mountain, Pen Cerrig-calch
and Pen Allt-mawr

Starting Point: Small car park on a minor road near Neuadd Fawr.

Access: Via road signed to Llanbedr from Crickhowell which is followed for 3 miles, ignoring the turn to Llanbedr. Located just beyond bridge over a stream at a sharp loop in the lane a quarter of a mile short of Neuadd Fawr.

Distance: 8¼ miles.

Detail: Five-mile horseshoe ridge, once height has been gained.

Map: 1:25,000 Outdoor Leisure Map No. 13.

This walk is exceptionally well endowed with extensive views virtually throughout its entire course and readers who have sampled some of the earlier expeditions will recognise old friends.

The Walk

Note: a permitted path provides an alternative start to this walk. From the layby, follow the lane back over the bridge to find a permitted path signed to the right. Head up the bank to a stile and, with the field boundary to your right, climb to a stile; cross a narrow lane to a further stile. Go forward with a wood to your left to reach a stile in a stone wall and a bracken-covered hillside. Turn left with the right-of-way continuing to meet up with the route from Rhosyn (Green Cottage).

From the layby, head back in the direction of Crickhowell with the lane, looking across the valley to forest and hills – perhaps with minute walkers or riders silhouetted upon the sky line. In three-quarters of a mile take the path on the right passing a cottage named Rhosyn (some maps may still show this as Green Cottage). This is a wide track running between hedges but with views opening to the wider world as height is steadily gained.

A gate set across the path may be locked and will have to be climbed, be-

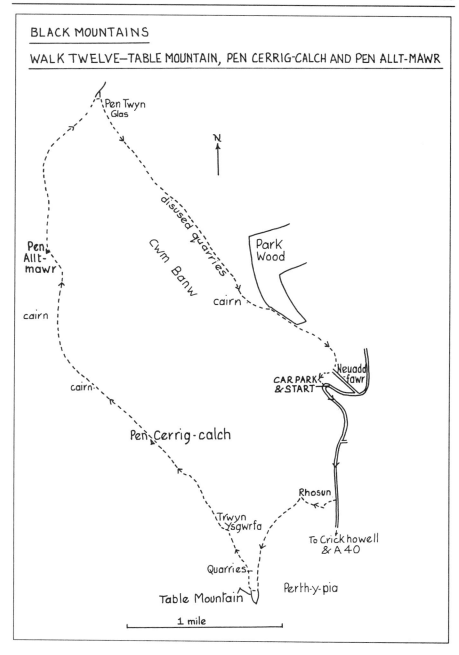

BLACK MOUNTAINS

WALK TWELVE—TABLE MOUNTAIN, PEN CERRIG-CALCH AND PEN ALLT-MAWR

yond this the path swings to the right and a quarter of a mile from the road a further gate leads to the open hillside.

Bear a little right on the rising path and in 60 paces turn sharp left on a clear path heading west of south. (Ignore the right turn towards Pen Cerrig-calch). The grassy path is followed through bracken with the tiny village of Llanbedr and its church tower seen tucked under the hills. Beyond the village, to the south-east, the isolated Sugar Loaf commands attention.

In a quarter of a mile the path follows the line of a wall, to your left, but parts company with it after 200 yards. There is a division of paths at this point, take the left fork with the path returning to the wall as it comes in at an angle from the left. From here go forward slight diagonally right, (roughly southwards), on a less distinct path for 600 yards crossing several small streams and passing disused quarries a little higher to your right.

When you draw level with the footpath rising on your left from Perth-y-pia turn right to climb 50 yards into the quarry area. (Note – if you miss this turn and continue for 200 yards towards a line of conifers you will meet a distinct path, where you turn sharply right to enter the quarry area).

If you wish to include Table Mountain and the Crug Hywell hill fort, after which Crickhowell is named, take the clear track westwards. The Iron Age fort set on the 1480 ft summit of the mountain can also be reached by other paths north of the town. From the northern end of Table Mountain continue with the clear track which runs towards Trwyn Ysgwrfa and rejoins the route from the old quarries as described in the next paragraph.

At the top of the short pull up to the quarry area, turn right through the old workings, heading directly to the southern end of the Pen Cerrig-calch ridge where a nose juts forward – Trwyn Ysgwrfa. Beyond the quarry area a grassy path will be seen climbing ahead. When well up the slope the path splits, fork left towards the nose, cross a small stream and then follow the boot-worn treads up the steep hillside. Meet a wide path coming in from the right, then turn left to continue to the viewpoint on Trwyn Ysgwrfa. (Note this track has taken an easier course winding round the hill and could have been followed by turning right at the split instead of left).

Now the views are wide ranging. Far below, the Usk Valley can be traced, with the river appearing here and there. To the right of Ta-

Table Mountain and the hills beyond the Usk.

ble Mountain are the white and grey buildings of Crickhowell and its thirteen-arched bridge. Beyond lies the nearby village of Llangattock, set between the Usk and the Monmouthshire and Brecon Canal. Rising above the village are the much quarried limestone hills where the scarp edges have been resculptured to provide the flux needed for the furnaces of the South Wales iron works. The pool lying high on Mynydd Llangatwg that may catch the light is Pwll Gwy-rhoc. Llandbedr lies far below in its setting of green fields and neat hedges a perfect design for a model village and toy farmyard. Sugar Loaf then Ysgyryd Fawr lie to the south-east and the radio masts beyond the summit of the Blorenge stand out like matchstick men. The north-east is bounded by the long ridge rising from the Grwyne Fechan Valley with Pen y Gadair Fawr and Waun Fach in sight for much of this walk.

Following the Usk westwards the valley splits, Dyffryn Crawnon hemmed in by Mynydd Llangynidr and Tor y Foel and then the Talybont Valley. Onward then to the Brecon Beacons with the distinctive shapes of Corn Du and Pen y Fan. Nearer to us, the long curve of the hill on which we stand leads on to the crags of Darren.

From Trwyn Ysgwrfa take the path which rises west of north heading for the triangulation point on Pen Cerrig-calch with improving views to the Beacons. In about a quarter of a mile, the paths divide. Take the right fork with the path still rising and leading through a vast jumble of scattered rock, the limestone from which the mountain gets its name. A cairn is reached, here the path continues along the edge of what looks like the aftermath of a hailstorm of great ferocity, with stones of record-breaking size. This carries on to reach the trig point on the 2300 ft summit, now with the Waun Fach ridge fully revealed.

From the summit continue north-west and in 100 yards passing a large bad weather shelter constructed from the ample supply of stones. Further shelters will be found at intervals along the plateau which is followed on its eastern side – a very exposed route which catches the wind from whichever direction it blows. From here, there is an excellent track all the way to the next landmark – Pen Allt-mawr – a mile and a half away.

The path descends a little, then falls sharply over an exposed limestone edge. There is a division of paths, take the one on the right which is seen running clear ahead with a cairn to mark the way as it continues close to the eastern scarp edge. There are fine airy views from here, not only to the other ridge but spying down upon the little secret valley of Cwm Banw. Ravens hunt round the limestone crags behind you and ahead the sun glints off the stony path.

Pen Allt-mawr, (2359 ft) too has its triangulation point, and no wonder for it commands a wide view, which is particularly fine to the north.

A view that is thrust upon the walker as he climbs the last few feet – suddenly laid out before him in one great magnificent gesture. The long sturdy isolated ridge of Mynydd Troed rises quickly from the valley of the Rhiangol and Cwm Sorgwm. Castell Dinas stands on the other side of the pass that heads from Talgarth to Crickhowell and, beyond it, the sharp spiny bank of Y Grib runs eastwards along the northern scarp of the Black Mountains. There are further views through the gap onwards to the Wye Valley and the distant Radnorshire hills.

Gliders swish through the hills here at impressive speed, often curving in closely at eye level with the walker and you may get a friendly wave from the pilot sheltered behind his perspex window.

There is a sharp descent from Pen Allt-mawr: northwards at first but gradually swinging a little to the right as the path runs over the spur to link with Pen Twyn Glas, effectively blocking Cwm Banw. The path, having lost nearly 300 feet in height, climbs again to pass a little under an unnamed "bump", then curving north-eastwards to gain the higher ground a little to the north of the summit of Pen Twyn Glas. Then swing right to Pen Twyn Glas with its small cairn.

From the 2119 ft summit, head generally south-easterly along the falling ridge (towards Sugar Loaf) for a mile and a half, eventually passing through abandoned quarries and on to the distinctive cairn (as described in walk eleven).

This is a minor ridge from which its larger brethren may be surveyed. Waun Fach on the one side and the almost oppressive heights of Pen Cerrig-calch and Pen Allt-mawr just traversed frowning down on you from the right.

From the cairn take the path forward left soon to join a track coming in from the left where swing right descending towards the trees. Pass over a stile in the wall and follow the outside edge of the forest on a falling track, bearing left with the forest after a short distance. In 200 yards the forest falls back; maintain your direction over the field to a further stone wall which leads via a gateway to a stony track. Descend with the track for 300 yards, passing a skeleton of an ancient tree, bereft of most of its limbs and stripped of its bark, a stark white ghost – a little eerie even in the full light of day.

At a bend in the track take the permissive path signposted right. Once over the stile, go forward for 40 paces, then sharp left descending towards a stream and in 100 yards swing left by a large oak to return to the car park.

The Black Mountains
– Walk Thirteen:
Pen y Gadair Fawr and Waun Fach

Starting Point: Small car park on the minor road near Neuadd Fawr.

Access: Leave Crickhowell on the road signed to Llanbedr and follow it northward for 3 miles ignoring the turn to Llanbedr. The parking place is found just beyond the bridge over the stream at a sharp loop in the lane.

Distance: 13 miles.

Detail: One sustained climb, wild moorland, and a long steady descent through the Grwyne Fechan valley.

Map: 1:25,000 Outdoor Leisure Map No. 13.

This walk includes Waun Fach, the highest point of the Black Mountains, but it can scarcely be called a peak. The high, featureless and sometimes soggy moorland plateau may cause some uncertainties in wayfinding at times of limited visibility and compass work may be required. Better, by far, to reserve this outing for a day with the promise of good weather. The initial climb to the ridge affords excellent views which can be quite stunning in the full light of an autumn day.

The Walk

From the car park continue with the lane for just short of a mile until the No Through Road sign is met near the gate to Cwm Farm. Here turn right on the lane which descends sharply and in 100 yards turn left on the signed public footpath, a broad track which soon crosses a stream.

About 50 yards beyond the stream the track divides; take the right fork which is found just beyond Brook Cottage. The track climbs steadily through woodland, broadleaf and conifer, and in 300 yards swings to the left. The path now follows the inside edge of the wood, the second leg of a

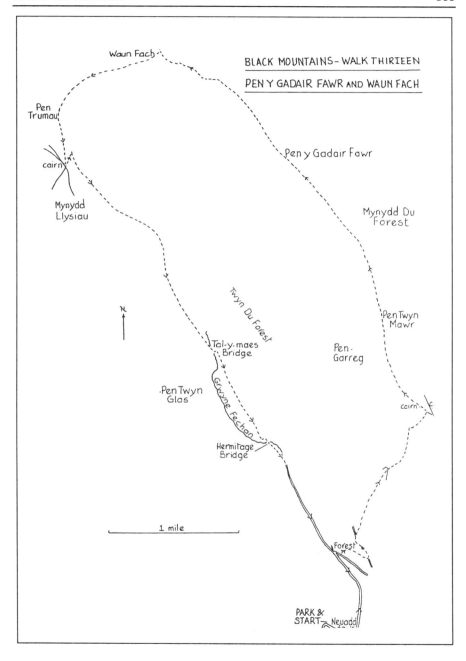

Waun Fach

BLACK MOUNTAINS – WALK THIRTEEN
PEN Y GADAIR FAWR AND WAUN FACH

Pen
Trumau

cairn

Pen y Gadair Fawr

Mynydd
Llysiau

Mynydd Du
Forest

N

Twyn Du Forest

Pen Twyn
Mawr

Tal-y-maes
Bridge

Pen·
Garreg

Pen Twyn
Glas

Gwyne Fechan

cairn

Hermitage
Bridge

1 mile

Forest

PARK &
START   Neuadd

zigzag. In 300 yards leave the track and bear right over a waymarked stile, still climbing on a wide, hedged track, north-easterly with the hills seen ahead. Digitalis lines the way in summer and fungi as autumn advances. The hedges disappear but maintain direction now with a stone wall on the left which soon gives way to a wire fence running along its skeletal remains.

Below is the white painted farm house of Nantyrychain – remote but picturesquely situated with its back to the forest. Beyond, the long ridges of Pen Cerrig-calch and Mynydd Llysiau are now in view and to your right the conifer plantations of Coetgae Mawr.

Continue on, passing through a gate into a further field keeping the wall on your left and thence over a stile to enter a plantation. A narrow but clear path follows the line of the wall through the darkness of the forest for 300 yards.

This is very comfortable walking with feet cushioned by a thick carpet of pine needles and the air lightly scented with the familiar essence used by the manufacturers of household disinfectants. Some interesting fungi are also to be seen here, a scatter of white umbrellas unfurled beneath the dark canopy of the forest, some in the typical ring formation.

Emerging into daylight, bear half right and in 50 yards cross a forest road and climb the bank to meet and cross a stile. You are now at the foot of a wide bowl formed by Pen Gwyllt Meirch to the right and the twin spurs of Pen Garreg to the left. The rim is some 525 feet above but the true top of the ridge is out of sight.

From the stile take the clear path seen running diagonally left, first through bracken then heather and bilberry. Maintain your general direction roughly parallel with the course of the stream seen to the left for 700 yards. Near a scatter of hawthorn, the track curves to the right, heading east then north-east to a narrow but clear crossing track in just under a quarter of a mile.

(Note this path is met about 70 paces north-west of the point where it leaves a broad ridge track. Should you have missed the turn by the hawthorn bushes, continue roughly parallel with the stream; you will meet the narrow crossing path marked by a cairn about 250 yards north-west of the recommended approach).

Turn left with the narrow path, north-westerly. A single conifer may be noted – an escapee from the now visible Mynydd Du Forest – making a solitary effort to survive. Whether it will succeed at this height without the protection of its companions is a matter of speculation. Maintain your direction with the track widening and climbing steadily to reach the summit cairn on Pen Twyn Mawr (2159 ft), in just under a mile after joining the ridge.

There are good all-round views of the upper profiles of the ridges. The Twyn Du Forest lies on the lower slopes to the left, to the right the Mynydd Du Forest has climbed fully to the summit from the floor of the Grwyne Fawr Valley. Forward Pen y Gadair Fawr can be seen, an unmistakable tent like structure pitched at 2625 ft on the rough moorland, one and a half miles to the north-west.

From the cairn take the path that runs a little west of north, over the intermittently soggy ground and nearing the forest. After half a mile, there is a division of paths – our way now lies more to the north-west, ignoring the short link to the good grassy track nearer to the forest. Continue with the narrow but well-walked path which, in 60 yards, runs close to the scanty

Typical Black Mountain scenery.

remains of a fence. It leads to the north-western tip of the forest area a little way to your right. From this point, the path continues clear ahead. It falls a little then rises with a last steep pull up to the centre of the "tent" to reach the cairn on the grassy summit.

From the summit of Pen y Gadair Fawr to the westward turn by the low concrete marker on Waun Fach is a little over a mile; as already mentioned, care is required in wayfinding in poor visibility. The path continues north-westerly, falling by a series of short dips into a sometimes soggy sump; once through this, the path runs clear enough as it rises towards the summit moorland of Waun Fach, 2660 ft, the less than dramatic highest point in the Black Mountains. There is an occasional modest cairn to help you on the way but the last section may not be distinct as you dodge round the peat hags.

The low concrete roundel at the northern end of Waun Fach carries a large red arrow marking the path that runs for nearly a mile over the spur to Pen Trumau. It travels at first a little south of west then curves to the south-west to reach the "nose" – a good viewpoint over the Grwyne Fechan Valley and to the steep slopes falling away from Waun Fach and Gadair Fawr.

Descend to the large cairn which marks the crossroad of paths on the saddle between Pen Trumau and the steep rise to Mynydd Llysiau. From this point you may take the high-level return route over Mynydd Llysiau and Pen Twyn Glas, as described in walk eleven.

The return by the Grwyne Fechan Valley provides an easy passage by a long falling path combined with excellent views. If you elect for this option take the path on the left as you face south which falls quickly down the hillside and in 200 yards swings sharp right. The clear path is now followed for two miles as it descends to the single-arched Tal-y-maes Bridge.

Once over the bridge climb to the gate, beyond which a grassy path continues diagonally right rising to a metal gate. Continue with the fence line on your left to a further gateway, passing a small plantation. Beyond a gate, join a metalled road which is followed for half a mile where it divides a little short of Hermitage Bridge. Take the right fork to cross the bridge and continue with the lane for nearly a mile to reach the junction near the gateway to Cwm Farm. Ignore the left fork and continue, retracing the steps of your outward route for three-quarters of a mile, passing Pentwyn, to return to your starting point.

The Black Mountains –
The Northern Escarpment

The northern escarpment has been partially explored, piecemeal fashion, in the pursuit of the various ridge walks but it deserves a place of its own for it offers double value. This comes in the shape of the fine end-to-end walk over the tops and the excellent views of the successive heights seen from the lower paths that run under the scarp edge. The network of paths that cross the open land that lies between the enclosed fields and the steep slopes are well worth ex-

The northern escarpment from Castell Dinas hill fort showing Mynydd Bychan and right Y Grib

ploring for from this lower level the mountains may be seen to better effect than from above. Some of these paths are indicated on the map, others not; for the most part, only tracks which appear on the map have been used to assist readers in relating the route description to the OS sheet.

The walks that follow split the scarp into two sections, each a complete walk in itself but may be used to provide one long outing. If transport can be arranged a linear walk along the scarp top is a practical proposition: Start from the Gospel Pass car park by the stone circle and follow the outward directions given in walk 14 as far as the top of Cwm Constab, then continue using the return directions as in walk 15 to the Pengenffordd car park – about seven and a half miles. By starting from the Black Hill car park, (Walk One) and following the ridge to the summit and on to Hay Bluff an extra four miles are added.

Combining the two walks by following the summits towards Pengenffordd and returning under the edge will produce a circuit of around 14 miles with shorter alternatives available – skipping the full Y Grib ridge for example.

The Black Mountains – Walk Fourteen: The Northern Escarpment – Hay Bluff – Rhiw Cwnstab

Starting Point: The stone circle car park north of Hay Bluff.

Access: Take the Hay-on-Wye – Abergavenny minor road to find the surfaced car park close by the stone circle 4½ miles south of Hay-on-Wye.

Distance: 9 miles.

Detail: The outward leg is initially a scarp edge switchback, the return under the hills is mainly level – both sections provide good views.

Map: 1:25,000 Outdoor Leisure Map No. 13.

Some minor wet black peaty patches on the tops give way to reddish mud on some sections of the lower paths – neither should inconvenience the booted walker and largely disappear in a dry summer.

The car park by the stone circle is popular with motorists making their way to or from Llanthony Priory. Picnic parties visit here and, in autumn, people with plastic bags are seen with downcast eyes, searching for mushrooms. A refreshment van is sometimes to be found here.

Hay Bluff may be hidden, for on the days when clouds are low it seems loathe to yield up its veil of secrecy; it is often the last to surrender to the gentle coaxings of an emerging sun or the more insistent persuasion of a freshening breeze. A lost world where man may appear to be an unwelcome guest but, for the walker confident of his navigation, a place of deep fascination as he dips in and out of the swirling mists.

The Walk

From the car park head a few yards up the road and take the track running diagonally left across the grassy, gorse dotted common, towards the summit of Hay Bluff. A steepening climb of a quarter of a mile will bring you to a distinct crossing path. Ahead an unmapped path, apparently of recent origin but already showing tell-tale signs of a future erosion problem, defies the breath snatching gradient and presses on to the top. But not for us this way, which seems set to produce an unsightly scar upon the hillside.

Take the crossing track climbing half right with rapidly improved views to Twmpa to the west and the wide arc of hills climbing out of the Wye Valley. A quarter of a mile of steady ascent leads to a path running along the scarp edge. To the left it leads in 300 yards to the summit triangulation point (2221 ft) but again refusing the invitation turn right following the clear path for almost a mile along Ffynnon y Parc.

There is a magnificent view down to the expansive commons and patchwork of wood and field and onward beyond the Wye Valley to the distant Radnorshire hills. There is even a brief snapshot of Hay and a glimpse of the often concealed river as it makes one of its characteristic meanders near Llowes.

As you advance, Twmpa becomes more prominent and the prospect opens up to other ridges: Darren Lwyd running away from Twmpa, Pen y Gadair Fawr with the highest of the Black Mountains moorland on Waun Fach. Further to the left will be seen the Bal Mawr ridge and the Blacksmith's Anvil close to the bridle way over the hills from Capel-y-ffin.

Height is steadily lost as the path dips towards the Gospel Pass; southwards, there is a long view of successive contours arching down to the Llanthony Valley. A timeless scene, dark and grey when in mist, a nostalgically atmospheric image to those accustomed to hill walking throughout the seasons.

The path meets the road close to the point where the Gospel Pass has climbed to its summit height of 1765 ft and starts its two and a half mile descent to Capel-y-ffin. From the road take the path almost immediately opposite. A clear but chameleon-like track which climbs 485 feet in three-quarters of a mile, with the ground underfoot changing from red mud, via a stony way to black peat and springy grass.

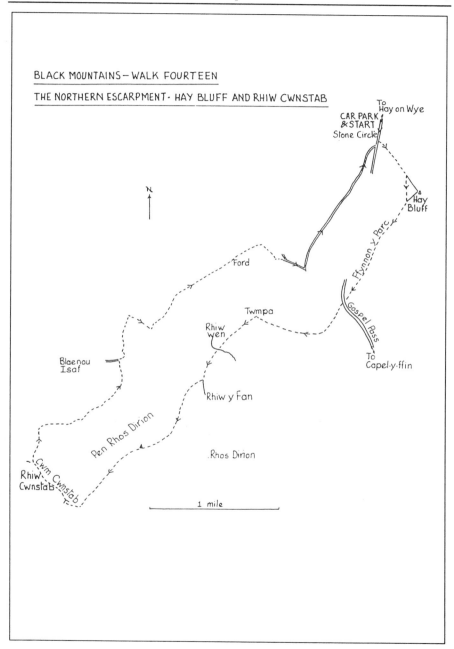

BLACK MOUNTAINS – WALK FOURTEEN

THE NORTHERN ESCARPMENT· HAY BLUFF AND RHIW CWNSTAB

Twmpa (2264 ft), less elegantly known as Lord Hereford's Knob, is announced not by a triangulation pillar but with a series of cairns. Another good viewpoint, not only to the Wye Valley but to the high rolling moorland spreading in every direction save north.

Lord Hereford's Knob (Twmpa) from Ffynnon y Parc - Hay Bluff.

From Twmpa continue south-westward over falling ground to cross the path from Rhiw Wen where a cairn marks the junction to Capel-y-ffin (Walk Three). Our direction remains unaltered making for the top of the deep ravine with its unnamed stream. Here the mountain has been stripped to the bone, revealing the deep red sandstone, a rouched curtain draped over the cliff.

Immediately beyond the cleft, the paths divide. One swings south over Rhiw y Fan and Rhos Dirion, but we remain faithful to the edge route (or as near as the path will allow) with a steady climb that in three-quarters of a mile reaches the triangulation point on Pen Rhos Dirion (2339 ft).

The view to the Wye Valley which has been lost for a while can be regained by walking a few steps northwards from the survey pillar. From the trig point continue with the clear moorland track which runs a little away from the scarp edge. Far ahead, the north end of Mynydd Troed just tips over the horizon and, as you approach the cairns marking the paths which converge at the top of Cwm Cwnstab, there is a long view towards the Grwyne Fawr Valley above which the full length of the Bal Mawr ridge is displayed.

This junction of paths at the top of the ravine is the turning point of the walk. From here descend north-west on the wide stony track set above the western side of the ravine. A nicely engineered way very rocky at first, which makes a zigzag passage which if fully pursed would carry you down to the western end of Wern Frank Wood. Half a mile from the summit, shortly after swinging left, a clear grassy path will be found on the right; descend northwards with this for a quarter of a mile.

There is now a fine view eastward along the scarp to Pen Rhos Dirion and Twmpa. A number of paths run under the hills but not all appear on the map, so the walk has been tailored to follow paths which can be identified on the 1:25,000 sheet even if this sometimes involves a slightly less direct route.

At the bottom of the slope swing right, dipping through a ravine to cross the stream issuing out of Cwm Cwnstab. From the opposite bank take the wide grassy track running north-eastward over the bracken-covered common. The path leads towards the wood seen ahead and continues a little away from its outside edge and crossing a series of streams falling off the slopes of Pen Rhos Dirion.

In about three-quarters of a mile, the fence line falls away. Bear diagonally left, northward, heading for the road ahead and crossing two paths in quick succession as you gradually draw near a wire fence and wooded area on your right.

Descend a small bank to turn right with the road and cross culverted streams. Ignore the first path on the right immediately beyond the stream and continue with the road for 40 paces; take the track diagonally right which climbs a bank and continues over bracken and gorse-covered moorland. In 100 yards the path improves and divides, take the left fork which in a quarter of a mile meets the road at a sharp angle. (A north/south track also makes a junction at this point).

Forget the road and swing half right, south-east, on the track with the fence line initially about 100 yards to your left but joined after crossing a small stream. About 400 yards from the road the direction changes to north-east as a stream carried in a deep gully is crossed. Several paths are seen rising from the opposite bank. Take the far left broad track and follow this for three-quarters of a mile with the fence line to your left, although from time to time it distances itself from your line of travel.

When the ford marked on the OS map is reached and crossed, the fence departs north-westerly; maintain your direction over the open common for a further 600 yards. The track now swings to the right heading towards the distant dip in the hills beneath Twmpa. Leave it after 300 yards taking the diagonally left track to a narrow metalled lane at a bend.

Turn right with the lane which is soon crossed by several streams. Beyond the fords the lane swings sharp left. A quiet pleasant way which is followed for a mile to return to your starting point. There are fine views to the long wall of Ffynnon y Parc to your right and retrospectively to the escarpment with Twmpa dominant.

The Black Mountains – Walk Fifteen: The Northern Escarpment Pengenffordd – Rhiw Cwnstab

Starting Point: Dinas car park.

Access: Three miles south of Talgarth via A479. Turn left at Pengenffordd on the single track road to reach layby parking in a quarter of a mile

Distance: 6 miles

Detail: The outward leg follows paths under the scarp edge, long ascent leads to a high-level return with wide views.

Map: 1:25,000 Outdoor Leisure Map No. 13.

The Walk

From the layby, go forward and turn right on the signed public footpath which passes Dinas Farm on your left. The path, indicated on the map as a RUPP (road used as a public path) climbs steadily to a Y-junction where you turn left through a metal gateway. From here a stony track runs north-eastward, following the line of a wall beyond which there is a panoramic view over the Wye Valley. To your right slopes climb steeply to build the long wall of the northern escarpment of the Black Mountains.

Keep with the track for a little under half a mile. When it starts to descend, leave it and take the track diagonally right, heading towards the deep scoop of Cwm y Nant and the fence line seen ahead.

A deep cleft dug by a stream is crossed. (Ignore the path which cuts through the mountains by Bwlch Bach ar Grib and the eastward track which climbs to the top of the scarp at the eastern end of Y Grib – but worth noting for future use). On reaching the fence follow the track which runs on the mountain side of the enclosures with a succession of streams flowing out of the impressive depths of Cwm y Nant.

The path leaves the fence line and heads up the bank above the ravine for about 60 yards then left to ford the stream. Once up the bank swing left to follow the track which runs under the pimple topped spur jutting out from Mynydd Bychan. This track runs a little higher than the fence line which, at this point, is about 150 yards to your left and provides a better viewpoint both forward to the steep slopes falling off the scarp edge and retrospectively to the distinctive outlines of the Brecon Beacons.

Your direction is now northwards. Half a mile on from Cwm y Nant the stream issuing out of Cwm Dwr-y-coed is crossed. There is a division of paths as you climb the bank, take the middle way, a clear track running through bracken. Further streams are crossed as you approach the southern end of Wern Frank Wood with a RUPP coming in from the left.

Climb the steep bank beyond the stream and swing half right on a clear, and at first rutted track which in a few yards divides. Take the right fork — a wide grassy path — the start of a three-quarters of a mile zigzag, 950 feet climb, to the top of the scarp.

As you turn to make the ascent there is an immediate improvement in the view with the widening of the arc. The Brecon Beacons and the Black Mountain in the west, the Wye Valley spread further for inspection and a great sweep of the hills encompassing Herefordshire, Shropshire and Powys. The Beacons apart the most easily identified of the distant "smudges" is the Radnor Forest signalled by the radio mast on Black Mixen.

The grass soon surrenders to a more travel-worn way of red earth, the flat pavement of the exposed bed-rock and ultimately a bruising jumble of small boulders as it climbs high above Cwm Cwnstab with its mini waterfalls. As you approach the top of the cwm the River Wye finally finds a visible place in the topography.

At the summit a scatter of cairns marks the meeting of ways. Coming in from the east is the track from Pen Rhos Dirion, (walk 14); ahead, a path rises before making the long descent down the Grwyne Fawr Valley (walk 8). A clear track runs in on the right from Y Das.

From the top of the cwm continue for a further 100 yards where a small cairn marks a path, at first indistinct, to the right. Take this route, south-west at first, trekking over the windswept moorland plateau, initially well away from the scarp edge as it cuts off the corners formed by the spurs of Y Das and Mynydd Bychan.

In about 100 yards, cross the track that leads to Pen y Manllwyn and

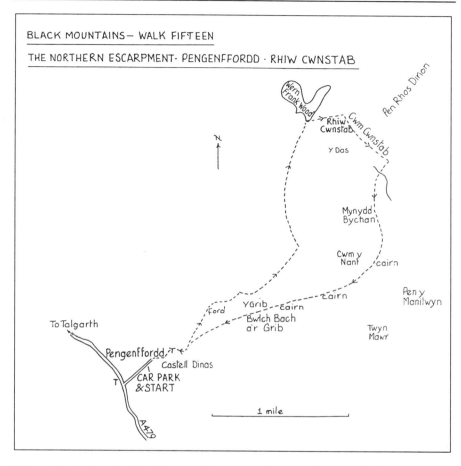

BLACK MOUNTAINS– WALK FIFTEEN

THE NORTHERN ESCARPMENT· PENGENFFORDD · RHIW CWNSTAB

Waun Fach (walk 10). Your path soon swings to the south then sweeps above the wide, deeply incised Cwm y Nant with its quite glorious views to the north (enjoyed from the opposite direction in walk 10).

In a mile and a quarter from the top of Cwm Cwnstab the paths again divide with a cairn marking the parting of the ways. (Ignore the descent under Y Grib and along the southern rim of Cwm y Nant unless you have decided to use it to shorten the full northern escarpment route suggested by combining elements of walks 14 and 15).

Continue over the ridge with views to the grounded white butterflies of the gliding club down to your right and to Pen Trumau and Pen Allt-mawr to your left; far below is the upper Rhiangoll Valley. Ahead lies the narrow Y Grib ridge – tautology for the bilingual since *crib* or *grib* translates variously as ridge or crest – and more distantly the sharply-cut Mynydd Troed.

Go forward along the tread passing a little rocky "fortress" to your right followed by a sharp descent on the rocky narrow way seen clear ahead. When the paths divide, take the right forward fork falling to cross over the pass – Bwlch Bach ar Grib.

Several paths will be noted running ahead (westward) along the northern flank of the ridge. They tend to peter out; take the second one from the top and, towards the end of the ridge, bear forward right on a now wide clear grassy path with Castell Dinas seen ahead.

The path runs obliquely towards the fence line to a gateway, beyond which you bear right and follow your initial outward route to return to your starting point.

Castell Dinas hill fort.

Useful Information

Accommodation

Camp and caravan sites, bunk houses, hostels, canal boats, self-catering cottages, farmhouse, bed and breakfast and full board are all available in the area. Abergavenny, Brecon, Crickhowell and Hay-on-Wye are obvious bases but B&B signs are to be found in the Talybont Valley, along the A40, the A470 and in the Llanthony Valley.

Tourist Information Centres can provide the latest lists and some offices offer a booking service. Many properties have been graded by the Wales Tourist Board, who issue a free publication "Wales Touring Caravan and Camping" available from PO Box 1, Cardiff CF24 2XN.

Tourist Information Offices

(Note: Not all of these are open throughout the year).
Abergavenny
Swan Meadow, Cross Street, Abergavenny NP7 5HH, Tel: 01873 857588 (also serves as a National Park Centre).
Brecon
Cattle Market Car Park, Brecon Powys. LD3 9DA, Tel: 01874 622485. Brecon Beacons National Park Office, Watton Mount, Brecon. Powys LD3 7DF Tel: 01874 624437.
Brecon Beacons Mountain Centre, Libanus Brecon LD3 8ER, Tel: 01874 623366
Hay-on-Wye
The Craft Centre, Main Car Park, Hay-on-Wye, Powys HR3 5AE, Tel: 01497 820144
Hereford
1 King Street, Hereford HR4 9BW, Tel: 01432 268430.
Merthyr Tydfil
14a, Glebeland St, Merthyr Tydfil CF47 8AU, Tel: 01685 379884

Travel

Wales Tourist Board issues a free publication "Wales Bus, Rail and Tourist Map and Guide" available from the Board at PO Box 1, Cardiff CF24 2XN.

Places of Interest and Other Activities

(This is a brief sampling – for a full list of current activities – fishing, hang-gliding, canal boating, canoeing etc., apply to the appropriate Tourist Information Office).

Pony Trekking: There are a number of centres, particularly in the Capel-y-ffin, Llanthony and The Forest area of the Black Mountains – refer local advertising or Tourist Information Centres.

Abergavenny – St Mary's Church, Castle remains and local museum.

Blaenavon – The Big Pit mining museum, Blaenavon Ironworks.

Brecon – Cathedral, Brecknock Museum, South Wales Borderers Museum.

Capel-y-ffin – The tiny village church and Father Ignatius monastery.

Hay-on-Wye – For book browsers.

Libanus Mountain Centre – Information, picnic site, guided walks programme etc.

Llanthony – Priory ruins and picnic site.

Tretower Court – Fortified manor house and earlier castle.

Path Problems

In the event of problems arising, complaints, (or indeed compliments) on signing, obstructions etc, should be reported to the appropriate authority.

Most of the walks are contained within the boundaries of the Brecon Beacons National Park. The Park Authority has responsibility for public rights of way in the Gwent part of the park. It is not responsible for the Powys section of the park although it carries out most of the work in this area. Powys CC say that problems can be reported either directly to them or to the National Park Office. A small section of the book falls within Herefordshire, contact addresses are given below. Some Tourist Information Offices will take note of footpath complaints and pass them on to those responsible.

Brecon Beacons National Park Office, 7 Glamorgan Street, Brecon, Powys LD3 7DP, Tel 01874 624437.

Powys CC Rights of Way Officer, County Hall, Llandrindod Wells LD1 5LG, Tel 01597 826000

Herefordshire County Council Rights of Way Dept, Bath Street, Hereford. Tel 01432 260572

As mentioned in the opening chapter, there are many well-used paths which are not, strictly speaking, rights of way. I am informed by the Park Authority that there have been generally few difficulties for walkers in the open hill area. Any problem areas I have become aware of during the compilation of this book have been excluded.

Finally – a word of warning – the car parks in the area are not free from the attentions of thieves – be sure to lock your car and secure valuables in the boot.

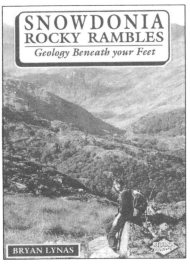

SNOWDONIA ROCKY RAMBLES
Geology Beneath your Feet

Bryan Lynas

This is a guidebook with a huge difference: learn about the rocks and scenery of Snowdonia as you enjoy some excellent rambles. Background text describes why the area looks as it does. Learn about the tremendous forces that shaped the earth, imagine huge volcanoes, picture the deep seas!

(£9.95)

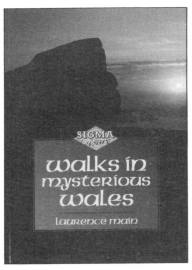

WALKS IN MYSTERIOUS WALES

Laurence Main

Follow the spirit paths of Wales - visit the most sacred and secret sites and discover ancient traditions of this historic country in the company of a leading expert. And, while you're discovering Welsh heritage, enjoy some excellent walks across the length and breadth of the country.

(£6.95)